Mad Tales from th

Mad Tales from the Raj

Colonial Psychiatry in South Asia, 1800–58

Waltraud Ernst

ANTHEM PRESS
LONDON · NEW YORK · DELHI

Anthem Press
An imprint of Wimbledon Publishing Company
www.anthempress.com

This edition first published in UK and USA 2010
by ANTHEM PRESS
75-76 Blackfriars Road, London SE1 8HA, UK
or PO Box 9779, London SW19 7ZG, UK
and
244 Madison Ave. #116, New York, NY 10016, USA

First published in the UK by Routledge 1991

Cover image 'View of Bombay Harbour, taken from the Island of Kolaba, 1833'
reproduced by permission of the Oriental and India Office Records,
British Library, London

British Library Cataloguing in Publication Data
A catalogue record for this book is available from the British Library.

Library of Congress Cataloging in Publication Data
A catalog record for this book has been requested.

ISBN-13: 978 1 84331 881 1 (Hbk)
ISBN-10: 1 84331 881 4 (Hbk)

ISBN-13: 978 1 84331 868 2 (Pbk)
ISBN-10: 1 84331 868 7 (Pbk)

ISBN-13: 978 1 84331 897 2 (eBook)
ISBN-10: 1 84331 897 0 (eBook)

Thrown Away

And some are sulky, while some will plunge.
[So ho! Steady! Stand still, you!]
Some you must gentle, and some you must lunge.
[There! There! Who wants to kill you?]
Some – there are losses in every trade –
Will break their hearts ere bitted and made,
Will fight like fiends as the rope cuts hard,
And die dumb-mad in the breaking-yard.

'Toolungala Stockyard Chorus'

… Now India is a place beyond all others where one must not take things too seriously – the mid-day sun always excepted…

But [a] Boy – the tale is as old as the Hills – came out, and took all things seriously. He was pretty and was petted. He took the pettings seriously, and fretted over women not worth saddling a pony to call upon. He found his new free life in India very good. It does look attractive in the beginning, from a subaltern's point of view – all ponies, partners, dancing, and so on. He tasted it as the puppy tastes the soap.

Only he came late to the eating, with a grown set of teeth. He had no sense of balance – just like the puppy – and could not understand why he was not treated with the consideration he received under his father's roof. This hurt his feelings.

He quarrelled with other boys and, being sensitive to the marrow, remembered these quarrels, and they excited him. He found whist, and gymkhanas, and things of that kind (meant to amuse one after office) good; but he took them seriously too, just as seriously as he took the 'head' that followed after drink. He lost his money over whist and gymkhanas because they were new to him.…

This unbridled licence in amusements not worth the trouble of breaking line for, much less rioting over, endured for six months – all through one cold weather – and then we thought that the heat and the knowledge of having lost his money and health and lamed his horses would sober The Boy down, and he would stand steady. In ninety-nine cases out of a hundred this would have happened. You can see the principle working in any Indian Station. But this particular case fell through because The Boy was sensitive and took things seriously – as I may have said some seven times before. Of course, we could not tell how his excesses struck him personally. They were nothing very heartbreaking or above the average… But he must have taken another view altogether, and have believed himself ruined beyond redemption. His Colonel talked to him severely when the cold weather ended. That made him more wretched than ever; and it was only an ordinary 'Colonel's wigging'!…

The thing that kicked the beam in The Boy's mind was a remark that a woman made when he was talking to her. There is no use in repeating it, for it was only a cruel little sentence, rapped out before thinking, that made him flush to the roots of his hair. He kept himself to himself for three days, and then put in for two days' leave to go shooting near a Canal Engineer's Rest House about thirty miles out. He got his leave, and that night at Mess was noisier and more offensive than ever. He said that he was 'going to shoot big game', and left at half-past ten o'clock in an *ekka*. Partridge – which was the only thing a man could get near the Rest House – is not big game; so every one laughed…

Rudyard Kipling, *Plain Tales from the Hills*

TABLE OF CONTENTS

LIST OF ILLUSTRATIONS

PREFACE AND INTRODUCTION
TO THE REVISED EDITION

When *Mad Tales from the Raj* was first published in 1991, few historians worked on colonial psychiatry and medicine. It took another four years before McCulloch explored the role of 'colonial psychiatry in Africa'.[1] The scope of these first two major studies could not have been more different. One focused on a subcontinent, South Asia, the other on a continent, Africa. *Mad Tales* was concerned with the early nineteenth, McCulloch's *Colonial Psychiatry* with the early twentieth century. Crucially, one paid particular attention to the theories and practices of British psychiatry in relation to Europeans in India, while the other assessed the role of western psychiatry in relation to colonial racism and Africans. Unsurprisingly, subsequent work on South Asia and Africa has expanded beyond both, focusing on the treatment of the Indian mentally ill during later periods and on case-studies of particular African regions respectively. The history of psychiatry within the context of various colonial settings has clearly come of age over the last two decades. Some reflection on how this reprint of *Mad Tales* can be located within a fast developing field of study is clearly indicated. This requires an appraisal of the historiographic reconfigurations and conceptual developments that have characterized South Asian medical history in recent years.[2]

In the 1980s, the study of medicine and colonialism was still in its infancy. Existing work drew on Fanon whose seminal book *Black Skins, White Masks* had been made available in a new English edition in 1986. He had warned against colonialism's 'separatist and regionalist' strategies.[3] Work in the emerging Fanonian tradition tended to produce generalizing and often psychoanalytically framed accounts of the 'condition' of colonizer and colonized. These deliberately avoided explicit critique of any lack of local focus and issues of 'subalternity'. Authors sometimes came dangerously close to reifying practitioners' and historians' sweeping stereotypes of whole regions' alleged mental predispositions and abnormalities. This was typical of work both on 'the African mind' and on 'the East's' and 'the West's' assumed characteristic features. The main proponent of this kind of approach in South

Asia, Ashis Nandy, had developed in the early 1970s a vernacular Indian version of Fanon's negritude in his *The Intimate Enemy*.[4] He argued the case of what Spivak later called 'strategic essentialism', the essentialization of the identities of the colonized to accentuate their shared interests as a disadvantaged group.[5] Nandy attempted to re-conceptualize into a subversive subject position of resistance Fanon's trope of the submissive and self-deprecating psychological and ideological position that is shared by all who have been (self-) identified as coloured/black people.

These kinds of agency formation in Fanon's and Nandy's rendering are intentionally aloof from the specifics of local circumstances and hence not easily reconciled with the tenets of richly contextualized histories of medicine in colonialism. Nandy's work became a popular anchor for medical histories framed in relation to the generalized dichotomy of colonizer and colonized.[6] Fanonian accounts, as also Foucaultian perspectives, appear to share the problematic tendency of stopping at the level of universal theory, so failing, deliberately, to accommodate the mundane minutiae of historical detail and evidence of diversity and heterogeneity on both sides of the bipolar divide. From Nandy's standpoint, the writing of the 'mythographies' of the oppressed is preferable to histories, as the latter are seen as objectifying and denigrating people's lived experiences. 'History' is castigated as an aspect of the 'Project Of Modernity' and its inherent alleged evils (of rationalization, homogenization, totalization and historicism). The divide between these two approaches is not irreconcilable. But it has continued to generate more heat than light in many scholarly debates in the field of colonial medicine.

From the late 1990s, the field expanded considerably. Many British historians working on medicine in South Asia have succumbed to the creative allure and analytical potential of the 'literary turn' and deconstructionist, subaltern and 'post'-approaches, especially as represented in the work of US-based Indian scholars such as Bhabha (Harvard), Spivak and Chakrabarty (Chicago).[6] The re-discovery of Foucaultian paradigms also guaranteed a continued engagement with power and hence with the colonial dimension of 'colonial medicine'. This emphasis sometimes worked to the detriment of 'medicine'. But it persisted, despite the fact that, as early as the 1970s and 1980s, discourse analyses had been shown to be limiting and potentially reductionist by scholars in France and Germany.[7] The engagement with discourses of power, attempts at textual deconstruction and crossovers to literary theory have certainly made some historical writing more complex, even to the point of incomprehensibility. Debates are replete with colourful and obscure terms and linguistic oddities. Within this broader context, research came to be skewed in one particular direction and at times, so it seems, scholars put the cart before the horse. Instead of locating the subject matter (medicine) within the wider social context (colonialism), they have critiqued colonialism through the lens of medicine.

It is of course important to assess the role of medicine in the making of the colonial state and identities. However, there is a tendency to reduce the analysis of the wider social context to the single dimension of colonial hegemony and resistance to it. Once medicine within a colonial context is abridged to its colonial provenance, it tends to deny political and social agency to people ('colonial subjects' in postcolonial lingo), in and against colonial structures. If medicine is construed as determined mainly by the agenda of colonialism, at the cost of other social dimensions, it results in incongruously mono-dimensional histories. There is more to medicine within a colonial setting than the discourse of colonialism – even when the limelight is on 'governmentality', 'hegemony' and 'colonial identities' as well as their companion counterparts: 'resistance', 'ambiguity' and the 'subaltern'.

It is doubtful whether the continued over-emphasis on the 'colonial', or, in its more recent version, the 'post' in postcolonial approaches to the history of colonial medicine can move us forward. Rather than probing *only* the specificities of 'the colonial' in British India and the role of medicine as a tool of empire, scholars may need to focus *also* on its provenance and the commonalities with the very context from which it originated: post-Enlightenment, capitalist Britain. It is necessary to consider the social and political contexts that framed British medical policies in India. These would include specific measures of state intervention, such as the 1858 Medical Act, which enshrined particular medical approaches as the single orthodoxy, sidelining heterodox practitioners and 'quacks'. The marginalization of indigenous Unani and Ayurvedic experts in the period up to the 1920s, in particular, as well as the rhetorical condemnation of folk and tribal practitioners in India more generally, is well in line with the denigration of heterodoxies such as homoeopathy, balneology and 'itinerant' practitioners, snake oil sellers and 'Sequahs' in Britain.

As in *Mad Tales*, we need to take into account policies that, although not specifically 'medical', nevertheless shaped the ways disadvantaged strata were being treated by 'the rulers' in the metropole: the Poor Law Amendment Act of 1834, for example, the debates on indoor relief, the principle of 'less eligibility' and the severe conditions in workhouses designed to be repulsive to those ground up by the wheels of a thriving (and periodically crisis-ridden) capitalist economy.[8] The prolonged discussions by the various provincial governments in British India on the merits and financial feasibility of institutional relief for poor Europeans and Indians in India were clearly fuelled by similar debates on the propriety and financial cost of indoor relief for paupers and the labouring poor in England and Wales.

In *Mad Tales*, the tenor of such measures was shown to have resonated in the territories newly annexed, 'pacified' and 'administered' by military force on behalf of the British Crown by a trading company keen on maintaining a competitive advantage during the dawn of imperialism around the globe. Alongside a plethora of measures, such as the Public Health Acts of 1848, 1875 and 1936 and the intimidating, gendered and punitive Contagious Diseases Acts of 1864, 1866 and 1869, medicine in Britain itself was not entirely devoid of those very issues of state power, professional hegemony and discrimination against the lower classes and women that have been identified as being at the core of medicine in the colonies. The development of 'metropolitan' (London) medical institutions along with large-scale hospitals and asylums in large county towns has its equivalent in British establishments in the colonial metropolises of Calcuttta (Kolkata), Bombay (Mumbai) and Madras (Chennai) alongside 'provincial' institutions in the various regions.[9] Finally, in Britain as in British India we can discern a plural or mixed economy of health care provision flourishing during a period when interventionist state measures prevailed happily alongside *laissez-faire* policies. This resulted in a multiplicity of public, private, voluntary and philanthropic institutions, services and informal indigenous practices.

Getting historians of colonial medicine to look West as well as East has certain potential dangers. An over-emphasis on British 'blueprints' and similarities between metropolitan and colonial medicine in South Asia may tend to mirror, reify and even excuse the ideology of colonial and Western supremacy and the hardships caused by British military expansion and cultural hegemony. Researchers attuned to the dire circumstances of colonialism in South Asia have for decades rightly critiqued the enduring ideology of British rule as 'gentlemanly', 'noble' and 'beneficial', pointing at the legitimating and stabilizing role of medicine and education in the pursuit of imperial supremacy and economic exploitation. They have highlighted the violence, dislocation and marginalization in societies under colonial rule. Whether this is matched in metropolitan society is highly contestable. The poor and 'subaltern' in the British Isles have clearly suffered hardship, too, in the face of the 'potato' famine in Ireland[9] and during such infamous repressive actions as the Highland Clearances,[10] deportations and hangings in response to the Swing Riots of 1830,[11] and the Peterloo massacre.[12] It is conceptually problematic and morally fraught to accentuate systemic commonalities between the situation in colonial South Asia and metropolitan Britain at the expense of their structural differences. Nevertheless, as highlighted in *Mad Tales*, it is important to keep in mind one of the main trajectories that connect the two; as V. G. Kiernan put it: 'Discontented native in the colonies, labour agitator in the mills, were the same serpent in alternate disguises. Much of the talk about the barbarism or darkness of the outer world...was a transmuted fear of the masses at home.'[13]

In the light of the wider commonalities and differences between Britain and colonial India, it is vital to be as cognizant of the specific history of colonial South Asia as of the economic and social history of Britain itself. To date, research on colonial medicine that unpicks those various intertwined threads of British and South Asian history on the levels of the 'mythographies' and discourses of modernity and identity, and in regard to the range of diverse policies and historical experiences in different localities, is still underdeveloped; the twain still hardly ever meet. Scholars favouring one or the other approach find it difficult to overcome their conceptual exclusiveness. They may also have a quite catholic belief in the putative irreconcilability of 'Theory' with 'proper History' or of 'Intellectual History' and 'Institutional History'. Clearly it takes both aspects to complete a critical, conceptually informed and well-evidenced history of colonial medicine. Some postcolonial theorists, historians of ideas and scholars of intellectual history may see this as coming too close for theoretical comfort to a wide-ranging, critical-integrative social history. Less conceptually minded historians of the Anglo-Saxon school of thought on their part might fear that 'Theory' might trump empirical evidence. The vital reconciliation between those two positions is still pending.

The intention of *Mad Tales* was to highlight the role of Western, institution-based psychiatry in the justification of British rule as a 'noble cause' and in the preservation of the prestige of the ruling race through institutionalization and repatriation of the European mentally ill. The wide-ranging source base consisted of government proceedings, medical case reports, contemporary publications, diaries and literary material. A multi-disciplinary perspective, commensurate with my training in politics, sociology, psychology, medical history and the history of South Asia was employed to explore various levels of analysis including: literary representations of madness and life in the 'Orient'; colonial politics; institutional policies; medical professionalization; patients' life stories; and medical theories and practices. The focus was primarily, though not exclusively, on European mental patients. No attempt was made to rigorously explore the fate of the Indian mentally ill and the various indigenous modes of treatment. The aim was to deconstruct the myth of Empire as a noble cause and burden for the British, questioning some of the stereotypical 'heat and dust' representations that continued to fuel the lucrative market in Britain for Raj novels, films and decorative memorabilia during the 1970s and 1980s.

Early-twenty-first century authors, in contrast, tend to concern themselves more explicitly with the assessment of 'indigenous medicine' – on its own terms as an important component of the wider field of health care provision flourishing alongside the range of orthodox and heterodox medical approaches brought along by the colonizers. This previously neglected aspect of history of medicine continues to be seen by some historians as belonging within medical and historical anthropology. Indigenous medicine of course always formed the background of historical discussion about colonial medicine. However, following the dictum established by the rhetoric of British colonial medicine itself, indigenous ways of healing were often conceptualized as the 'Other' to colonial medicine (or 'Western', 'cosmopolitan' or 'biomedicine'). This tended to relegate indigenous ways of healing implicitly to a referential if not subordinate, or 'subaltern', position. Indigenous medicine may also have become further reified in its marginalization and 'othered' position by historians' continued preoccupations with hegemony, control and discursive subjugation. The frequent employment of dualities such as Western—Eastern and modern—traditional further accentuated and enshrined as valid entities ideologically problematic East—West, traditions—modernity bifurcations that had flourished concomitant on the upsurge of Enlightenment ideas in Europe.

The ideological premises underlying these popular East—West binaries were tackled in *Mad Tales*. The juxtaposition of colonial/Western/modern with indigenous/Eastern/traditional was a main reference point also of one of the earliest publications in the field of colonial medicine, *Indigenous Societies and Colonial Medicine*.[14] These earlier works signalled the need to open up the skewed self-referential focus on 'colonial medicine' and bring into view the indigenous component. This fitted in with ambitions among historians of South Asia more generally to recover the 'subaltern' perspective and retrieve the voice of those who had previously not been heard – an allegedly new agenda that had in fact been derived from social history as developed earlier, during the 1960s and '70s. If *Mad Tales* were to be written again now, it is likely that it would encompass both indigenous and Western perspectives, focusing on Indian and European mental patients in equal measure and exploring vernacular Indian sources alongside British ones. It would be able to do so with confidence not least because previous work provided the groundwork for and neglected engagement with 'indigenous' components. Historiographic fashions come and go in waves, with a tendency for new generations of scholars to throw out the baby with the bathwater and to reinvent the wheel.

The reprint of *Mad Tales* in a slightly revised version facilitates recognition that colonialism is a relational concept and its comprehensive assessment requires us to move beyond simplistic 'East and West' bifurcations. *Mad Tales* did this by dismantling various myths about the adverse effects of the Orient on Europeans, and showing how the different, prevalent medical paradigms variously underpinned, informed or challenged public preconceptions and colonial ideologies. It also focused on a group of 'subalterns' that did not until more recent re-assessments qualify for this label: the mentally ill and in particular the poor mad men and women of European descent who had hardly ever before made it into the histories about those 'who ruled India' – not even in their sane state. Being subjected to social exclusion, prejudice and discrimination was not the prerogative of the colonized alone. This does not justify colonialism, but it makes the investigation of phenomena such as medicine and psychiatry within colonial settings more multifaceted and complex.

Oxford, December 2009

Chapter 1

INTRODUCTION:
COLONIZING THE MIND

Some 'mysterious transformation' is said to have affected Westerners once they
proceeded East of Suez.[1] The view that experience of life in an alien Eastern
country set travellers and expatriates apart from their fellow countrymen was
common amongst those who reflected upon the effect on generations of
Europeans of life in the Orient. So much was the East—West encounter
perceived as leaving its mark on people's personality that those who had lived in
the Orient for some time were regarded as a 'distinct species'. Their peculiar
views, attitudes and behaviour were both excused and explained by reference
to life abroad and on return to Europe they were treated 'either with awed
bewilderment or humorous ridicule'. What sparked off this 'mysterious
transformation' has since the eighteenth century been subject to speculation.
Some assumed that it was the alien environment that was to blame, in that polite
manners and sociable behaviour were 'jungled out' of those exposed to
prolonged life in the tropical forests and arid plains of the Indian peninsula.[2]
Others were inclined to see the lack of 'restraint of parents, relatives and friends'
as upsetting the mental balance and emotional inhibition of a number of those
young, predominantly male, *griffins*, or green newcomers who, being 'thrown
together' with others of their age, became 'violent and intractable'.[3] Yet others
went so far as to deny that anybody who lacked first-hand experience of life in
the East could 'ever really understand what it was like' – thus pre-empting any
attempt by the uninitiated to come to grips with the factors that are said to have
made all expatriates 'members of one great family, aliens under one sky'.[4]

A variety of explanations have been advanced for the European's alleged
character change under conditions of 'heat and dust' in the Orient's plains
and hills, but one has commonly been agreed upon: travellers, merchants,
diplomats and soldiers from a variety of different lands were susceptible to it.
The psychological metamorphosis of the English has, nevertheless, been
characterized as quite distinct from the process of cultural adaptation incurred
by members of other European nations. It was the 'insularity of the English
character' (said to have been as marked in the eighteenth as in the nineteenth

century), which made the English 'persist on their customs and habits of life even in most unfavourable circumstances'.[5] The melancholic traits to which the 'inhabitants of England were doomed by geographic accident'[6] were said to have made it difficult for them to endure solitude[7] or 'the ordinary misfortunes of existence'[8] – let alone unfamiliar circumstances 'in a clime so remote from their own'.[9] The upshot was the exacerbation of those character traits which in the British Isles were merely looked upon as signs of eccentricity or a sensitive or nervous disposition. In India, so it has been suggested, they turned into 'an exaggerated and vulgarised edition', 'modified by climatic conditions' and more visibly and literally out-of-place because of the lack of 'the tradition and continuity of English society'.[10]

Despite variation in emphasis, these images of what made the English in the Orient a 'species apart' have been reproduced time and again during the last three centuries. Such popular speculations, taken up and dwelled on by many a scholar, may contain a grain of truth. Exposure to unfamiliar cultural conditions can have psychological consequences characterized by a variety of emotional and behavioural coping strategies, of which anxiety, anger or depression are the most common, usually followed by a tendency to either over-adapt or respond aggressively to the alien environment.[11] It is certainly the case that British government officials and military officers in India remained in most circumstances aloof from their Indian subjects. The observation that, unlike the English, the French and the Portuguese cultivated a less detached and socially inhibited stance towards Eastern people may indicate existing differences in the way in which members of different nations react to unfamiliar situations.

However, the flaw in these hackneyed images of the nature of British colonial rule in India is that they are redolent of an Anglo-centric ideology. Most British accounts of the alleged 'mysterious transformation' of character during the British Raj are in fact limited to the *English*, ignoring the contribution of the Scottish, Irish and Welsh to British—Indian policy and social life. The possibility of highly diverse impacts of the 'alien' on Britons of different regional backgrounds and diverse behavioural responses to life in the East is neglected. The omissions are not merely the result of an imprecise use of language. They indicate a tendency in the fictional, biographic and historical literature to present the British—Indian encounter in an almost exclusively English light and from the point of view of those 'who ruled India'.

Apart from a few authors such as the ubiquitous Kipling, most widely-read accounts of the British in India have conveyed the myth that colonial society was differentiated simply into an English ruling elite, on the one hand,[12] and an amorphous (though reputedly gorgeously colourful) mass of 'native' subjects, higgledy-piggledy subsumed under the label of 'Mohamedans', on the other.[13] Such oversimplification has served a still lingering imperial ideology, fixed on the idea of a homogeneous ruling class, united by a noble vision and devoted with supreme self-confidence to the colonizing duty. This ethnically and socially discrete ruling class in India emerged, so the story has it, towards the end of the eighteenth century, when the time came for

> the flowering, the highest peak perhaps in the lofty range of what the English have done, when a handful of our countrymen, by the integrity of their character and with not much else to help them, gave to many millions for the first time for some centuries the idea that a ruler might be concerned with their well-being.[14]

Oversimplification is however not a monopoly of imperial ideology and 'heat and dust' fiction. A number of anti-imperialist accounts have in their turn been based on the similarly sweeping assumption that colonial society could simply be dichotomized into the white colonialist elite on the one hand and exploited 'natives' on the other. In fact, the European community in areas administered by the East India Company by the end of the eighteenth century consisted of people with an English, Scottish, Irish, or Welsh regional background, interspersed with people of mixed race and nationals of European countries who had been taken on in recruiting depots on the Continent, as well as a large number belonging to what could be called the poor or lower classes. For people of such a variety of cultural and social backgrounds life in India not only had different meanings, but also affected them in many different ways. For a start the decision to sign on for a passage to India in the service of the East India Company would in the case of lower-class soldiers most typically have been induced by harsh economic necessity and the guarded hope that some of the recruiting sergeants' promises might come true. Members of the upper or middle classes, in contrast, while not devoid of material motivation, would at least potentially have been in a position more socially advantageous to reflection on the East's serendipitous material bounties as well as its spiritual and cultural offerings and mysteries. Lacking interest in the latter, they could indeed be free – to the extent of snobbish ennui – to engage in social activities characteristic of decadent upper-class life at home.

An ordinary lower-class man of 20, with the optimistic name of John Luck, for example, who left his native Lincolnshire during the trade recession of 1838 for military duty in the East India Company's artillery, as he was 'not happy trayiling in the contry for work', admitted after three years of service in Bengal: 'i ham so ancious to se my dear native home agane...as i know too well this country would soon kill me', imploring his mother 'if for ever o a due, sell not my ole close'.[15] He would clearly have experienced the East quite differently from, say, Lord Auckland, governor-general from 1835 to 1842, who was according to his sister mainly 'bored' by the splendid extravaganzas and ceremonial spectacles put on for his amusement while touring North India.[16]

Such a comparison of the experiences of selected lower-class persons with those of particular gentlemen is not meant to imply that social class was the only factor affecting people's varied responses to life in a foreign land. It certainly is important to point out that the popular image of life in the East tends to concentrate on the whims and woes of the upper classes. Such colonial myths need to be refuted by reference to historical accounts reflecting the variety and complexity of responses to the politics of colonial rule and the alien Indian environment and culture. However, whilst being 'to the manner born' will have made a satisfying experience and successful career in the East more probable, it certainly did not guarantee it. On the other hand, there are examples of ordinary soldiers who, contrary to popular opinion, appreciated Indian ways of life and preferred residence in India to that in the British Isles. Some members of the higher classes too seemed attracted to Eastern ways of thinking and living, while others failed utterly to gain fame or fortune.

Take the case of Richard C., on military duty in South India from 1856 to 1858. He often felt 'quite desperate and ill', confessing that he was 'so very very lonely' and 'heartily sick of the Army'; in fact he was sure that he would 'never do any good in it'.[17] Yet he also emphasized that he liked India 'amazingly' and thought it a 'glorious country'. Similarly, seven soldiers petitioned the Madras government to be allowed to stay on after between 12 and 26 years service in the King's or the Company's troops. They argued that they would feel like aliens with no economic future back in England. They also wished to stay with their Indian wives and the children borne by them.[18] Captain Thomas Williamson, author of the famous *East-India Vade-Mecum; or, Complete Guide to Gentlemen intended for the Civil, Military, or Naval Service of the Honorable East India Company*, expressed his positive view of Indians in 1810 when he pointed out that they were a 'race whose intellectual qualities, whatever may be said by ignorant or designing men, are at least on a par with those of Europeans'.[19]

Clearly, sentiments towards 'natives' were varied. Similarly, life in India stood for many different things for people who planned to spend some time in the East. For some it was the land of mysteries or of regrets, of unfulfilled hopes, the El Dorado of their dreams, the land of milk and honey, where a prosperous career could easily be made, or else an escape from economic hardship or professional failure at home, a self-imposed punishment for past personal wrongdoings, a challenge or a place where passions and predilections could be uninhibitedly expressed. In the face of such great variety of individual dreams, expectations, hopes, longings and projections it seems vital to resist any temptation to judge all expatriates' perceptions and experiences of India alike, or in consideration of their class background alone.

Any account of the way in which mentally ill members of the European community in British India were treated during the days of the East India Company will consequently have to go beyond the idealized and one-sided popular image of British social life during the Raj. It will also have to open up the narrow and myopic 'medical gaze' and attempt to lend a voice to the people hidden behind mental institutions' 'silent inmate inventories', by squarely locating medical and psychological treatments and patients' life stories within their wider, socio-cultural and economic context.[20]

What then were the features characteristic of British social life in India? The social context within which, say, the young writer, or clerk, from Europe would have found himself on arrival in one of the ports of entry in India towards the middle of the eighteenth century was that of a small, closely-knit and hierarchically-organized expatriate community, living in quarters separate from Indian society. In Bengal the European community in the 1750s amounted to no more than 76 civil servants of the Company, 500 officers and soldiers, and about 100 non-official Europeans.[21] At the top-end of this enclave of Europeans would be the president or governor who was, according to one historian

> a being poised midway…between heaven and earth, to the settlement a sort of tutelary deity, to Indian ambassadors and durbars the representative of the Britannic Majesty, and to the Directors [of the Company] an inveterate object of suspicion…he kept up considerable state; he never went abroad without being attended by eighty armed peons as well as English guards, with two Union flags carried before him and 'country musick enough to frighten a stranger into belief the men were mad'.[22]

Close behind the governor, with less regal splendour but still high social status, followed the members of his council and other senior Company officials, military officers, merchants and planters. The next social layer of the European settlement consisted of soldiers, sailors and minor Company servants who lived a life apart from the civilian and military elite and spent their time off-duty, so it is reported, amongst their own kind, frequenting the nearby punch-houses.[23] The professions would be sparsely represented with but a few chaplains, surgeons, barristers and teachers. Similarly, European women would be scarce. This lack was compensated for by the then widespread and socially accepted practice of 'domiciling' Indian women.[24] Although the British kept aloof from Indian society even during this reputedly open-minded century of the Enlightenment, they were willing to adopt those Indian customs that made life more comfortable and luxurious.[25] The maintenance of Indian mistresses was one such example of the Europeans' 'Indianization'; it was generally approved of until early in the nineteenth century and had obvious financial advantages.

European wives were costly to keep, so that it was much cheaper to support 'a whole zenana of Indians than the extravagance of one English lady'.[26] The small sum of between £2 and £4 per month attendant upon concubinage was considered to have been more compatible with the financial means of an average civil servant or officer.[27] A British wife, in contrast, would require dressmakers, hairdressers, ladies' maids and other major expenses, which could add up to about £300 per year. This tidy sum, it was held, pressed hard even on a husband in respectable circumstances who would in addition have to spend about £600 per annum for a middle-class establishment in Calcutta, even without the luxury of a garden-house in the cooler suburbs and exclusive of a carriage and frequent parties. Given the small official salaries of £27 for a writer and £132 for a council member, most civil and military servants would not have been able to keep a European woman in any style.

Financial considerations alone could, however, not have accounted for the attraction of Indian wives. Even the cost of an average household that allowed a young bachelor to live, if not in luxury then at least, in reasonable style, would exceed by far his regular income. But then, at this early period hardly any Company servant relied on the small salary afforded to him by the Company's directors. After all, the second part of the eighteenth century was the time when really big fortunes could be made in the East and Company officials, military officers or free merchants, traders and planters would return to Britain as 'nabobs'. The 1750s and 1760s in particular were considered the heyday of 'unbridled corruption and bribery'.[28] Although not all members of the European community shared in the acquisition of the East's bounty (and could therefore afford to engage in excess and merrymaking), an ostentatious lifestyle that would have made the dazzling entertainments of Vauxhall and the Brighton Pavilion appear as mere side-shows was characteristic of the *nouveaux riches* in the East.

Although it might seem that such conspicuous parading of one's riches copied Oriental rulers' extravagance and splendour, this lifestyle was not dissimilar to that of the upper classes in late eighteenth-century England. William Hickey, a man of 'amorous disposition' and familiar with the 'nocturnal dissoluteness' in London and Calcutta, travelled India during the reign of King George III and depicted in knowledgeable detail orgiastic banquets (and subsequent hangovers).[29] In his *Memoirs* he pointed out the striking similarity between the entertainments of polite and moneyed society in London and Calcutta, describing both as 'frivolous, unscrupulous, immersed in fashion, addicted to heavy eating, hard drinking, gambling, and duelling'. A crucial difference between the grandee in London and the 'nabob' in India was, however, that the latter was typically middle class in origin and upper class only in manners. This fact may have contributed to some of the sneering on the part of refined English society at the 'nabob' who returned to England and bought himself into parliament and upper-class social circles.

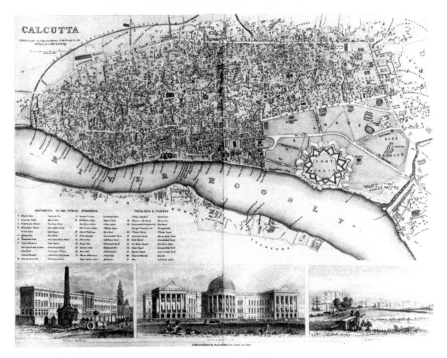

Figure 1. Map of Calcutta, showing the Lunatic Asylum, 1842.

In the decades leading up to the Indian revolt or Mutiny of 1857 things changed drastically. For one thing, the Company's involvement in the East gradually shifted from commerce to the expansion and administration of territory. Along with this change (which has been poignantly characterized as a shift from 'mere collection of *loot*...to orderly, if still burdensome, administration') went an increase in the number of Europeans and a growing sense of community spirit that set the British ever more apart from Indian social circles.[30] In consequence of the earlier Pitt's Act of 1784, which established a joint government of Company and Crown, and the crucial administrative reforms undertaken during the 1780s and 1790s by Cornwallis, service for the Company had gradually become a more adequately paid career and less of an adventure and opportunity to accumulate a fortune by corruption, patronage and connection. Lord Cornwallis, who 'came as a reformer of abuses with plenary powers, and brought with him the viewpoint of the India House and Whitehall, no previous knowledge of the country, and a lack of that imaginative sympathy which would have made up for his ignorance', achieved not only a gradual purge of corruption but a widening of the racial and social gulf.[31] His phrase 'every native of Hindustan, I verily believe, is corrupt', became an oft-quoted guiding principle of the British approach to racial relations during the nineteenth century and succinctly expressed the growing belief that Indian society was intrinsically inferior and had to be subordinated to European guidance – a view that culminated in the Victorians' ideology of their civilizing mission.

Concomitant on sharpened racial discrimination, the maintenance of the rulers' prestige became a central theme of government policy and of the conduct of the affairs of daily life. Indians were, for example, excluded from higher government offices and, on the more petty, though psychologically and symbolically important, level of social etiquette, chairs were no longer provided for spectators in legal courts and, in Calcutta, Company clerks 'expected every Indian to salute them'.[32] The social hierarchy amongst the European community was no less affected by the ruling class's concern to preserve the image of the British character. The behaviour of the steadily increasing number of lower-class Europeans (soldiers, sailors and minor clerks and, in particular, down-and-outs such as deserters, vagabonds, prostitutes and drunkards) consequently became a concern, which was to be complemented and sustained during the nineteenth century by the ideology of the Poor Law, namely 'not so much…to help the unfortunate as to stigmatize the self-confessed failures of society'.[33] When, for example, soldiers left military stations and started roaming the country, they drew the uneasy attention of civil authorities and political agents. Although it was asserted that 'pecuniary aid is easily given in these cases', the main problem was rather that of 'lowering the European Character in the eyes of the Natives'.[34] Consequently the measure most frequently resorted to was punishment and incarceration in India, followed, ultimately, by deportation back to England.

The Company's organizational development from the middle of the eighteenth century to the Indian revolt of 1857 was both reflected in and sustained by a corresponding shift in social and racial relations and in a reorganization of the European community itself. It had been the male adventurers and merchants who came to India for commerce during the age of Enlightenment; it was the soldiers and administrators who accompanied them to annex and govern from the end of the eighteenth century onwards; and finally it was European women who increasingly rounded off the hitherto more or less exclusively male European community during the nineteenth century. According to Spear's contentious judgement, they brought with them their 'insular whims and prejudices, which no official contact with Indians or iron compulsion of loneliness ever tempted them to abandon'.[35]

The expatriate community grew increasingly socially stratified and by the middle of the nineteenth century had developed all the symptoms of full-blown racial discrimination and social prejudice. This attitude of 'airy disdain and flippant contempt' had a 'background of fear which an unknown and incalculable environment is liable to excite in everyone' – a fear which may partly account for the ferocity with which racial and social relations were imbued.

Indians were referred to in a derogatory way as 'blacks', 'natives' and 'brutes', if not in the court room, at least in the drawing room.[36] Whilst all Europeans were equally subjected to English constitutional principles, special legal provision was made to restrict the influx to India of poor Europeans and to punish and deport undesirable down-and-outs who were considered to 'vex, harass and perplex the weak natives' and to thereby harm the high regard in which the British liked to think they were held by Indians.[37]

A particular social development, occasioned by the colonial nature of the British presence in India, was the emergence of a strong military barrack culture, sharply separated from the small European stations' civil lines and the towns. Shortly after the Indian Revolt, in 1861, the European civilian population in the whole of India only amounted to one fourth of the military community (namely 22,556 and 84,083, respectively, exclusive of 19,306 women).[38] A further important factor in the development of racial and social relations was the steadily growing number of people of mixed race. Although British—Indian liaisons had in the eighteenth century implicitly been approved of, the offspring of such relations had to a certain extent always been considered a socially undesirable consequence – unless the children's father was of high rank and would provide for the more fair-skinned of his descendants to be educated in England.[39] With these exceptions, by the beginning of the nineteenth century people of mixed race lived on the margins of both Indian and European society. This was despite the fact that they made up a numerically significant part of the cities' populations. In 1822, the Christian population of Calcutta, for example, was calculated to have been 13,138, of which only 2,254 were Europeans, while the rest, namely 10,884, were of Eurasian extraction.[40]

The changes that occurred between 1750 and 1858 in the Company's administration and in European social life were considerable. Although greatly furthered by contingent circumstances and stimulated and modified by local peculiarities, these developments were no less significant than (nor were they independent of) the changes that occurred in Britain during the same period. Any sensible investigation of the 'transformation of the British character' in the East would consequently have to take cognizance of its historical dimension and would further have to see it as being as much a product of developments in the imperial motherland as of Indian specificities. In an attempt to characterize the changes in the British policy towards India the historian Stokes pointed out that

> the loose, tolerant attitude of [Company officials such as] Clive and Hastings, their readiness to admire and work through Indian institutions, their practical grasp of the British position, unclouded by sentiments of racial superiority or a sense of mission, were ultimately the reflection of eighteenth-century England. The transformation of the Englishman from

nabob to sahib was also fundamentally an English and not an Indian transformation, however much events assisted the process. Indian experience undoubtedly hardened certain traits in the English character, but for their origin one needs to penetrate to the genesis of the nineteenth-century English middle class, and to the hidden springs setting its type.[41]

In fact, the popular contemporary self-perception, too, changed from seeing the British involvement in the East as a commercial enterprise and lucrative adventure under taxing environmental conditions, to emphasising the 'white man's burden' amongst alien peoples. It thus expressed and grasped one aspect of the changing socio-economic and historical conditions. What both the Georgian merchant-adventurers and the Victorian civil and military servants shared and bore, either with the equanimity or fervid over-statement typical of their respective period, was the burden of their own social culture which they could not but carry along with them.

Chapter 2

MADNESS AND THE POLITICS
OF COLONIAL RULE

Ideological Positions

Writings on the Raj have often been fuelled by political interests and nearly always served some particular ideological purpose. James Mill's *History of British India* (1817), for example, represents an early attempt by a distinguished protagonist of utilitarianism and advocate of Enlightenment values, to support the idea of converting the Indian subcontinent into a nation governed by reason, fed by European knowledge. There were many other accounts, both preceding and following Mill's description of pre-European India as a society characterized by despotic rule and barbarism, and of Europeans' corruption and idle high living, or devotion to duty. Some of these were immersed in a vision of the spirit of Enlightenment or, more militantly, the *pax Britannica* spreading across the Indian peninsula. They sometimes described gruesome details of violent Indian customs (such as the burning of widows, mutilation of children and strangling of travellers) as evidence for the necessity of Westernization. Others (of which there were fewer) attempted to adduce evidence as to why India was no longer 'worth keeping'.

Diversity of view is however not confined to the realms of fiction and scientific writing. It is in fact liable to characterize any but the most totalitarian political system. Government officials in India, too, espoused a variety of different ideological positions, personal interests and idiosyncrasies. Discussion of any aspect of government is therefore bound to reflect this, and lunacy policy is no exception. Take the example of the Bombay council during Lord Falkland's governorship in the late 1840s and early 1850s. Although unsavoury allusions to officials' private lives and embezzlement of funds were then made less frequently than only a few decades earlier, when Bombay society sweltered in a 'continual effervescence of scandal and gossip', tempers were still inflamed by widely different opinions on the province's administration, especially in acerbic discussions of the allocation of public resources.[1] A long dispute ensued, for example, when improved institutional facilities were mooted for the province's chronically insane. 'The subject of lunacy', asserted Falkland in 1850, 'is engaging and will continue to engage my attention'.[2] The governor, renowned for his humanitarian attitude and very much liked by both the European and Parsi communities, strongly supported a proposal by the medical authorities to provide 'amply' and 'on the most approved system' for the treatment of the province's lunatics. The other council members in contrast, mostly old India-hands of many years' standing (unlike Falkland, who had recently arrived from England), found such expense 'quite out of the question'. They held that more important areas needed government's attention and that 'in this and in many similar cases we have not merely to consider what is *desirable*, but what can be afforded'.[3] Consequently the plans for a new asylum in the province were put on ice despite numerous reports of the old premises' overcrowded conditions.

Disagreements between council members, governor, commander-in-chief, and governor-general were reflected in many dissenting minutes sent to England with the request for arbitration by the Company's London authorities. The Bombay government in particular appears to have had a long history of disagreement amongst its civil and military servants who were renowned for their 'intractable temper' and for only slowly developing from parochialists with 'minds of the average country town' to a more cosmopolitan and open-minded species of colonialists.[4] In some instances personality clashes and the tense atmosphere of a small closely-knit community of expatriates played a crucial role. Tempers were also aroused by ethnic tensions, with Irish, Scottish, Welsh and English officials accusing each other of jobbery and nepotism.

Henry Dundas, a Scotsman, for example, was influential on account of his position as president of the board of control, a parliamentary body set up in London in 1784 to supervise and direct the Company's civil and military policy in India, and, under Dundas's firm leadership, the ultimate arbiter of political decisions. He was accused of (and envied for) securing positions in the Company's employ for his favourites – a tendency which some ideologues of British colonialism nevertheless thought 'put India in his debt'.[5] A certain tension between military and civil servants, too, appears to have been a characteristic prolegomenon to policy making. Lord Dalhousie, governor-general from 1848 to 1856, for example, strongly disapproved of his commander-in-chief, Sir Charles Napier's, actions in the Punjab and finally accomplished not only his adversary's resignation but the establishment of the unequivocal superiority of the governor-general's position over that of the commander-in-chief.

It was not always financial prudence alone that led to antagonism and controversy. Nor was it simply personal grudges and nationalistic or professional chauvinism that could kindle administrators' passion. Some officials were seriously disposed to impressing their ideological position on India. This vast area of land, allegedly peopled with inferior races and subjected to despotic tyranny would, from the point of view of the Benthamite, liberal reformer or spiritual evangelical zealot, greatly benefit from the imposition of what some considered to be the most advanced and progressive socio-political regimes. Many ideologues consequently used their prominent position in the Company's administration to experiment with their favourite political brainchild.

John Stuart Mill and even more so his father James, for example, both important members of the Company's executive government in England, were in a position to leave a decided utilitarian mark on a number of relevant matters of policy making. James Mill was himself very much aware of this privileged situation, describing in a somewhat inflated fashion his job as being the 'internal government of 60 millions of people'.[6] In a similar vein his son, John Stuart Mill, proclaimed that his father had to a great extent been able to 'throw into his draft of despatches, and to carry through the ordeal of the court of directors and board of control, without having their force much weakened, his real opinions on Indian subjects'.[7] A Benthamite influence seeped through to India – and not only via despatches from England.

On the Indian side of government, too, utilitarianism had its advocates. Lord Bentinck, for example, had, on occasion of a farewell dinner with a small distinguished circle of Utilitarians on the eve of his call to India as governor-general, been feasted on 'the pure milk of the Benthamite word' and was, on his arrival in Calcutta, advised by one of Bentham's disciples. Bentham consequently wrote to Bentinck full of joy that he felt as if 'the golden age of British India were lying before me'.[8] Similarly, Mountstuart Elphinstone, governor of Bombay from 1819 to 1827 (and close friend of Edward Strachey, a 'Utilitarian and Democrat by creed' and along with James Mill employed as assistant examiner in the India Office in London) put a distinct Benthamite mark on the administration of civil affairs in his province.[9] He was also a great advocate of Bentham's 'panopticon' idea and had been responsible for

Figure 2. View of Bombay Harbour, taken from the Island of Kolaba, 1833.

experiments with large-scale public institutions in Bombay nearly two decades before similar plans were considered for the supreme province of Bengal.

Utilitarianism did not only stand for the support of large institutions, although this was certainly a most important aspect during an era pregnant with what Foucault came to describe as the 'great confinement'. They favoured a centralized system of asylum provision in place of patchy measures such as had been previously implemented on a more or less *ad hoc* and uncoordinated basis and, as Bentham would have seen it, in a dilettante and not always rational way at the local level of colonial administration. Bentham himself did much to spur the lunacy reform movement in England, advocating not only the establishment of large-scale and specialized institutions, managed by experts and subject to regular control and inspection, but also a consolidated national lunacy policy based upon rational principles rather than discretionary decisions by non-experts. The system of lunacy provision that was to emerge in British India by the middle of the century owed a great deal to the Utilitarians' 'science of government'.

The surprisingly short discussion in 1820 about the erection of the Bombay Lunatic Asylum bears witness to this.[10] The decision to have an institution built that could lodge as many as 100 patients implied asylum construction on an unprecedented scale for the times. Sanction of such an ambitious project by both the Bombay council and the London authorities was remarkable, especially in a period when the provincial governments in India were expected by the Company to curtail public expenditure. The Bombay medical officers had initiated the proposal on grounds of its expected long-term cost-effectiveness and service efficiency. This met with the approval of both Elphinstone and his council, and the London officials, as it implied a less extensive and expensive system than the one that prevailed in Bengal. In Bengal several lunatic asylums for Indians existed in different parts of the province, in addition to a separate, private institution for Europeans in the capital.[11] Admittedly, other factors than merely a Benthamite disposition were at work in Bombay, such as a less distinct inclination in this province to separate Indians from Europeans and reluctance by officials to simply mimic the supreme province's policies as had recently been directed by the Company's authorities in London. A certain panopticon-enthusiasm is however easily discernible, despite the fact that the asylum on its completion in 1826 and, incidentally, on the eve of governor Elphinstone's departure from India, provided for only half the number of inmates for which it had originally been planned.[12]

The idea of 'panopticon' and the complementary principles of economies of scale and centralized and rationalized provision for the mentally ill was not put to rest though. In 1849/50 the question of whether lunacy provision ought to be decentralized and several small institutions built in the various provinces or whether one single receptacle near Bombay would be more cost-efficient and cure-effective was once again laid before the Bombay council.[13] This administrative and political question had become more pressing since the annexation of Sind and the Punjab, with new and vast areas of land and peoples with a culture of their own to be governed from Bombay. The Bombay medical board was still attuned to the 'panopticon' idea and therefore strongly in favour of large institutions, maintaining that 'more benefit at a moderate cost would be produced on a certain number of Insanes by their being accommodated and treated in large, rather than in small asylums'.[14]

In the event, and not uncharacteristically, the council failed to arrive at a joint decision and eventually shifted the matter back to London in 1853. The authorities there were strongly in favour of keeping the system – albeit on a more restricted scale – as it had developed until then, maintaining that financial prudence as much as common sense told against a single new large institution. How could a place possibly be found that would be 'central' enough in an area where transfer from remote districts to Bombay was almost as nonsensical as shifting lunatics all the way from London to St Petersburg?[15] The idea of 'mammoth' asylums and their centralized administration had been bred for Western Europe's industrialized centres and its more easily accessible and comparatively small hinterlands. In India, however, distances posed a challenging logistic problem. Too few lunatics of both European and Indian descent seen as fit subjects for institutionalization were dispersed over too large an area. Thus, unlike in Britain's industrialized urban conglomerates and rural centres, the 'panopticon' and with it a system of centralized asylum provision was not yet a practicable solution for colonial India. Consequently, several medium-sized establishments in the main centres of population were kept open, the smallest and most dilapidated ones were discontinued and the idea of a 'panopticon' was dropped – for the time being.

Utilitarians were not the only political visionaries who strove to realize their aspirations in India. An evangelical strain of thought was being nurtured by Charles Grant, a member of the 'Clapham Sect', who used his influence as director and chairman of the East India Company to ensure that India would be opened up for the civilizing mission. His pressure group succeeded in having India thrown open to the religious zeal of missionaries from 1813 onwards. He was also partially successful in – though not solely responsible for – the restrictions on the number of lower-class Europeans who were permitted to emigrate to or stay on in India. 'Low and licentious' Europeans, if let loose on the 'weak natives', would 'vex, harass and perplex' them, Grant argued, and would be detrimental to the ultimate noble aim of colonial rule of spreading 'our light and knowledge'.[16] Grant's argument appealed in its essence beyond militant evangelicals to many members of the respectable British community in India. They were keen to prevent destitute sailors, vagrants, deserters, lunatics and such like from becoming a 'threat and nuisance' on every street corner of the trim and neat European parts of their towns.[17] The policy of sending European lunatics back to England, which was made official for all provinces under British rule from 1818 onwards, owed much to Grant's street- and mind-cleaning mentality (notwithstanding the logistical problems it posed).[18]

Less proselytizingly than Grant, but no less effectively, a Whiggish mark was left by administrators such as Lord Auckland, who controlled Indian affairs in his capacity as governor-general from 1836 to 1842. In regard to lunacy policy he insisted on as little intervention by the state as possible. He consequently thwarted attempts by the Bengal medical board to get rid of the privately owned and managed European Lunatic Asylum and its stubborn proprietor who continually demanded greater latitude than the province's medical officers were willing to grant. Although the place served only as a temporary receptacle for patients awaiting a passage back to England, it constituted not only an essential element of the city's medical institutions but also a lucrative income source for its owner. At the time private ownership of asylums and instruments to ensure public control of their internal affairs were heatedly debated in England. Auckland's 'hands-off' policy was therefore somewhat out of step with recent trends in the metropolitan public health sector, where the powers of controlling bodies such as the commissioners in lunacy were in the process of being extended in an attempt to guarantee close surveillance of public institutions as well as of private entrepreneurs in the medical sector.

It took another decade, until 1856, and the more autocratic style of government of Lord Dalhousie, to impart to lunacy policy in Bengal, too, 'those great measures of internal improvement' which he was so 'desirous of promoting' during his term of office in British India.[19] In practice, Dalhousie put an end to the previous *laissez faire* approach in the Bengal 'mad-business'. He established a 'Government Lunatic Asylum' in Calcutta, which was to be supervised by an experienced medical officer, regulated by a strict set of rules and controlled not by a board of medicos (whose rambling discussions Dalhousie loathed and deemed unproductive) but by the province's single director-general.[20]

Bureaucracy, Corruption and Public Opinion

Different ideologies and styles of leadership resulted in a diverse patchwork of often contrary policies, not only at different times but also in the different provinces due to a lack of a single central government authority. This is evidenced clearly in the diverse approaches towards land taxation and settlement, and the varying extent to which the Indian peasantry suffered alienation from its means of livelihood. The lunacy policies in Madras, Bengal and Bombay, too, were varied and subject to continual reorganization. In England itself, the first half of the nineteenth century had yet to produce any unified treatment of the mentally ill. This was still the period of *laissez faire* with its mixed blessing of experiments and individual initiatives in the absence of restrictions by the state, on the one hand, and of rampant abuse of the mentally ill due to lack of public control, on the other. Neither in England nor in British India can we therefore assume the existence of *a* 'policy' in any coherent sense.

Nevertheless, some features were characteristic of all the European asylums in India – most derived from Great Britain, but others were more or less specific to a colonial version of British mental health policies. One such 'typically colonial' feature was the extent to which the colonial state controlled the setting up and intervention in the running of mental institutions, even during a period of *laissez-faire*. This is not to say that state control was by any means as centrally organized and allegedly all-encompassing as in, say, France, which has been described as the harbinger of the 'great confinement' in reference to the tendency of the emergent capitalist state to institutionalize the deviant strata of society. What the suggestion of an interventionist stance by the colonial state does imply though is that lunacy policy in India, whilst firmly rooted in the more temperate Anglo-Saxon tradition and insular idiosyncrasies, was not simply a poor imitation of English whims and social developments, but rather a colonial hybrid that was allowed to grow somewhat more luxuriant under tropical 'hothouse' conditions.

What then were British officialdom's measures towards the European mentally ill in India? In Madras, first attempts towards the clarification of authority structures in the administration of the asylum and rules about the extent to which it was subject to medical as well as government control had been made as early as 1808.[21] Similarly, the Bombay authorities made provision for the maintenance in the asylum of both military and civil employees of the Company (and even, from 1801, for individuals unconnected with it).[22] Rules for the internal management and public control of asylums were also drawn up in 1801. In Bengal the situation was less clear – mainly because here the only asylum for Europeans was left in private hands until almost the time of the Indian revolt of 1857. However, even in Bengal the policy of regularly shipping inmates back to Europe was implemented from 1818 onwards and some control, however restricted, was exercised over the asylum proprietors' regime of management and their admission and discharge practices. Long before, from 1788 onwards, lunatics of all sorts – albeit mostly those of purely European origin – were routinely admitted to the province's asylum and the expense for their maintenance was charged to the exchequer's accounts.[23] Moreover, because of the existence of medical boards vested with the immediate responsibility for the provinces' medical affairs and institutions, a system of public inspection had been more or less successfully in place in India from the late eighteenth century onwards, preceding the setting up of public watchdogs such as the 'commissioners in lunacy' in England by about half a century.

From today's stand-point it may well be held that measures such as the clarification of authority structures and the enforcement of rules about the relative place of medical and government control in the management of asylums are mundane matters that would characterize *any* organization at any time. Surely, the least a state or state-like organization would do was to provide and enforce the framework of rules within which institutions are to operate? However, if in the particular case of colonial lunacy policy the extent of the state's control is contrasted with policies 'at home' in England, things look quite different, as the Company practised interventionism at a time when reformers in England were still unsuccessfully campaigning for it.

The existence of routinized practices, regular inspection and more or less detailed regulations of course does not imply that in practice things went according to the book. Mismanagement, corruption and petty disputes were uncovered on several occasions. Corrupt practices and mediocre performance were, however, typical of all departments of government. The more important point here is that, notwithstanding petty scandals, the East India Company officially took charge of insane European subjects in India at a time when in England and Wales the central state's liability for the secure custody and medical treatment of the mentally ill was still under discussion and not realized until 1845. This important difference certainly owes much to a strong Scottish presence amongst colonial administrators with a typical Scottish brand of humanitarianism and state intervention. It is also due to the peculiar nature of colonial rule in the East Indies itself.

Towards the end of the eighteenth century the East India Company's administration of Indian affairs was gradually consolidated and the Company itself subjected to scrutiny by the British parliament through a board of control. There was to be no more trade without complementary civil and military measures. Military supremacy would ensure that British footholds in India could be upheld. Civil administration would be instrumental, as Grant argued, in diffusing 'the light and benign influence of the truth, the blessings of well-regulated society, the improvement and comforts of active industry' among Indian peoples who had 'long sunk in darkness, vice and misery'.[24] It would also guarantee the smooth functioning of small – albeit steadily enlarging – pockets of European settlements amongst an allegedly backward people. With the passing of Pitt's India Act and the Cornwallis Reforms and, finally, the abolition of the Company's trade monopolies in the East (in 1813 for China and in 1833 for India), the shift from commerce to government was nearly complete.

The Company's authorities in India gradually assumed the function of a 'pseudo-state' with a retinue of administrators, the forerunners of the 'heaven-born' members of the later civil service. The governors of Madras, Bombay and Bengal met regularly with their councils to discuss the various departments' policy matters and conveyed their minutes to London to await sanction by the court of directors. The court of directors in its function as the Company's governing body in turn despatched its decisions to India, after having them approved by the parliamentary board of control. These multiple levels of administration resulted in tension amongst officials at various points in the hierarchy. The subordination of this administration to the British state proper was maintained by the dependence of the renewal of the Company's royal charter every 20 years on the findings of a select committee specially installed to investigate the administration of East Indian affairs. Consequently, public opinion and parliament's approval were decisive factors for the survival of 'John Company's' rule in India. Areas of public concern such as the fate of lunatics tended to attract often critical attention. After all, the early nineteenth century was the period of humanitarian campaigns and social reforms, with celebrities such as William Wilberforce and Sir Andrew Halliday rousing middle-class public opinion in support of causes like the plight of slaves and the destitute and mentally ill in Britain and abroad. The Company's court of directors in London therefore was in principle desirous that the local governments in India introduced without delay the recommendations of select committees on lunacy – especially if the envisaged reforms did not constitute any additional major expense.

The 1815/16 select committee on the better regulation of madhouses in England was the most influential. It had originally been set up with the aim of controlling the infamous practice by private asylum owners of making the most of a 'free market in lunatics' then flourishing mainly because of the lack of public establishments for mentally ill paupers. A pressure group of philanthropists sought to reveal and prevent gross abuses such as came to light in an inquiry when an emaciated James Norris was found chained to the wall in a pitiful state in Bethlem Royal Hospital in 1814. During the course of the investigation strong evidence was provided of the 'filth, neglect and unthinking brutality' found to be typical of lower-class institutions.[25] There was no indication that up-market establishments that provided for a select number of well-to-do patients suffered from defects even remotely comparable to those endemic to pauper establishments. Abhorrent conditions were the doubtful privilege of the poor and were generally ignored by the wealthy. As Chadwick had it, the facts were 'as strange' to the wealthier classes 'as if related to foreigners or the natives of an unknown country'.[26]

Despite the conclusive evidence pointing to the necessity for 'better care to be taken of insane persons', the remedial measures proposed by the committee were not legally enforced.[27] The condition of lunatics in England therefore experienced as little improvement as it had following the previous select committee of 1808 when the erection of publicly funded county asylums was advised but not made compulsory. None of the 1815/16 committee's proposals, such as the creation of especially designed and publicly financed and controlled county asylums was implemented in England until 1845. In India, in contrast, some of the core proposals envisaged by the committees of 1808 and 1815/16 had been realized by the first two decades of the nineteenth century. (The presence at the Company's London end of reformist officials necessarily facilitated this process.) The abolition in 1817 of the practice of contracting-out the supply of asylum provisions to private entrepreneurs or medical officers is but one example. The advocacy in 1820 of a regime of 'non-restraint' is another.

Long before the committee of 1808 would recommend the construction of a public asylum in each of England's counties, a government asylum existed in Calcutta (albeit only until 1821) that admitted mentally ill Europeans of all social classes alongside Eurasians of the higher classes. Further, government asylums for Europeans in Bombay and Madras were opened alongside separate public institutions for Indians in Bengal during the first two decades of the nineteenth century.[28] Very much in contrast to asylums in England, both the institutions for Indians and those for Europeans were subject to public control, regardless of whether they were in private hands (like the Calcutta asylum from 1821 to 1856) or state-run (in Bombay and Madras). They had in theory to be visited regularly by a board of inspectors, and the superintendent, who had to be a medical professional or at least have routine medical assistance, was obliged to keep registers and case books. On special occasions visitors such as the governor-general and 'some of the highest authorities of Government' would be shown round on the premises, so that the general impression prevailed that the British in India were at least as humanitarian as, if not 'much further advanced than England'.[29]

When conditions in asylums in India had deteriorated towards the middle of the nineteenth century, the London authorities made their wish explicit that 'those valuable improvements in the treatment of Lunatics which have been introduced into European Asylums should, as far as possible, be made available for the benefit of the same unhappy class in India'.[30] This statement sums up the Company's official stance towards the mentally ill in India. The ruling classes in India, it appears, were eager to convey the image of an elite that was devoted to the welfare of its own and its subject peoples. Such an image was as important for the preservation of the expatriates' self-perception as superior and enlightened beings as it was for the British public's conviction that British colonial rule was a blessing for alien peoples.

Exposure of grievances like those endured by James Norris in London would have been unpalatable to the British and the expatriate community had it occurred in Calcutta among European asylum inmates. That is not to say that abuse of lunatics did not exist in British India. To the contrary, the government of Bengal, for example, had been alerted by reports of the 'numerous deaths' that occurred in some of the province's asylums for 'natives' due to insufficient institutional provision. It consequently installed a committee to inquire into the 'state and internal management of lunatic asylums'.[31] Circumstances very much akin to those in the worst kind of lower-class institutions in England were revealed and condemned by the authorities.[32] The crucial point was, however, that gross abuse was only detected (but rarely successfully acted upon) in the treatment of *Indians*. Notwithstanding the fact that the mortality of European second-class patients in the Bengal asylum, for example, had been nearly double that of the first class (reflecting the class-specific death-rates of the European community in India as a whole), Europeans seem to have enjoyed throughout the early part of the century conditions very much superior to those prevalent in the various districts' 'native lunatic asylums' and the Bombay and Madras asylums' 'native wings'.[33] If the humanitarian image of the British had to suffer somewhat, then it was in regard to the treatment of the Indian rather than the European mentally ill.

Whilst abuse of inmates and mismanagement of asylums was largely confined to the institutions for 'natives', malpractice was a phenomenon deeply embedded in almost all government departments. Corruptive practices not only had adverse effects on government finances but were in many cases also detrimental to patients' health and welfare. A typical and most consequential case was that of asylum and hospital contracts. Ever since the establishment of a lunatic asylum in Bengal some time prior to 1787, food provision, clothing and bedding were supplied by a private contractor, typically the asylum owner or medical officer on duty in the institution. This practice and with it the well-founded suspicion of large-scale embezzlement was well known among British officialdom in India. In hospitals, too, contractors had for decades made large profits by pocketing money for provision that had never reached patients: 'on some occasions at least the health and life of the Soldier was sacrificed to the avarice of the Surgeon'.[34]

Despite the authorities' familiarity with such 'very great abuses', not much was done to enforce more stringent regulations. For nearly three decades no steps had been taken to change lunatic asylums' supply system. This could partly to be blamed on ignorance or indifference, but it had also a personal dimension ever-present among government officials within the restricted circle of polite society in British India. Public servants wined and dined with the very same officers whose source of additional income they could eliminate by changes in public administration. Even *griffins* or newcomers who may at times have arrived in the East with the best intention at some future point to rectify ills and better the ways in which the Company's affairs were being administered, found it difficult to elevate themselves above the common practice of profiteering and favouritism. They after all had to nurture social contacts if they did not want to risk exclusion from social entertainments and the looming threat of loneliness and depression.

Charles Metcalfe, for example, who, romantically, regarded politics to be the 'most noble of professions', arrived in Calcutta in 1801.[35] Of the few events noteworthy enough to be entered in his diary during the first few weeks in town were regular dinners at 'Dr Dick's'.[36] Dick was the owner of the lunatic asylum and a well-known and influential medical practitioner with extensive private practice. No newcomer, however convinced of the heroic role of colonial politics, would have dined with ease at Dick's had he contemplated officially raising any serious allusion to the doubtful nature of some of his host's income sources.

There were nevertheless limits to the extent to which malpractice could be condoned by local public servants for prolonged periods. One such was set by the increasing scrutiny of the Company's officials and the parliamentary board of control in London. For example in 1816 the examiner in London got a whiff of potential corruption and demanded a change of system in Bengal.[37] It was recommended that the commissariat was to supply the Calcutta asylum's necessities against bills countersigned and checked by the medical board. Furthermore, the medical officer in charge of asylum inmates was no longer allowed to pursue additional occupations. Such attentiveness to the detail of asylum administration had been sparked off partly by public and parliamentary concern for lunatics in England, which peaked in 1815. It took however some time before government policy to curb corruptive practices was implemented well enough at all levels of asylum administration to be beyond public criticism – let alone, to have a positive effect on inmates' daily life. Changes in regulations alone could not guarantee improvements.

The extent to which any administrative reform would work on the spot was of course very much dependent on whether officers right down the hierarchy diligently carried out their superiors' instructions. The Company's employment practices did not encourage asylum personnel to see their job as a career rather than as an opportunity for additional earnings. Although salaries were kept on a comparatively high level, promotion prospects were erratic and unsatisfying to many. Further, the position of asylum superintendent was usually but one among several charges of a medical officer – and one that did not enjoy any particular kudos. It was only towards the end of the Company's rule, in the late 1850s, that double-incomes and corruption by government employees more generally came to an end.

Despite corruption and bad conditions in institutions for Indian patients right until the middle of the nineteenth century, the Company could claim that it had developed for its European lunatics a system of care, if not, as Sir Andrew Halliday proclaimed over-enthusiastically, 'much further advanced', at least very much the equal of the more salubrious institutions in the British Isles. It was to a great extent public opinion in England and parliament's scrutiny of civil administration in the East that helped to detect petty embezzlement and spurred reforms in lunacy provision. It remains to be assessed how such reforms were implemented and tailored to the specific needs of colonial rule. One conspicuous point is that officials were prepared to pursue interventionist policies in the colony in contrast to reluctance to promote a centralized and costly public health policy in Britain during this period. Even the great advocates of state intervention, James and John Stuart Mill, were in a critical note characterized by a Calcutta newspaper as 'demagogues at home' and 'despots abroad'.[38] It was alleged that they judged 'Indian questions by rules and standards the very opposite of those they employ to decide all other questions whatever'.

What was it that made civil servants opt for an interventionist style of government abroad whilst remaining liberal at home even in areas of policy making as marginal as lunacy policy? Officials in India worked, of course, in a completely different setting. The changing emphasis in colonial administration from, say, Hastings' injunction to 'adapt our Regulations to the Manners and Understanding of the People' to that of a Macaulay who wished to raise 'a class of persons Indian in colour and blood, but English in tastes, in opinions, in morals, and in intellect' accounted to a great extent for strict state control.[39] Such control was to be exerted not only over the Indian subject people but also over the European communities who were after all expected to provide the role models to which Indians were expected to aspire. Further, there was the widespread belief in the civilizing mission that justified centralization and nurtured reformist measures. India appealed to Enlightenment ideologues who saw their chance, as Wilberforce succinctly expressed it, 'to strike our roots into the soil by the gradual introduction and establishment of our own principles and opinions; of our laws, institutions, and manners'.[40] Western vanguard ideologies and political practices were in fact transplanted to the East but – and here it is important to quality Wilberforce's emphatic statement somewhat – they were modified to better fit with the precepts of colonial control.

The Sick, the Poor and the Mad

There were further characteristics at work relating to the social make-up of European colonial society itself that encouraged state control. The British – in particular the lower classes – had found a peculiar freedom in India: freedom from a sense of belonging to the place where they spent much of their working lives, from family ties and the attentions of the guardians of the poor. For military servants, army hierarchy and regimental pride sometimes helped to create (despite ingrained regionalist and religious tension among the English, Welsh, Scots and Irish) a real *esprit de corps*. Among civilians, social cohesion and community spirit were kept alive by the continuous struggle to maintain distance from an unfamiliar Indian environment. Despite the ruling elite's endeavours to recreate English social life in the East and to cling together in small exclusive social circles, the European community was largely devoid of either family support or, in the case of the lower classes, parochial relief. There were no overseers of the poor who were by force of custom or law responsible for the care and control of European down-and-outs.

Polite society in places like Calcutta, Madras and Bombay made some effort to raise money for institutions such as orphanages, sailors' homes and hospitals for the poor. Lushington's account of Calcutta's missionary and charitable institutions in 1824 provides evidence of such private relief initiatives. The European community in Madras, too, was known for its initiation of social relief projects, while Europeans in Bombay were at pains to compete with the local Parsi community, who had a strong tradition of charity. The funds raised by subscriptions and collections were, however, never sufficient to provide for the steadily increasing number of poor whites who tended to take to the streets. Nor could funds invested in poor relief help to clear destitute 'natives' from European quarters in built-up areas or ameliorate to even the smallest extent the living conditions of the Indian poor. Absence of parish relief and the limitations of private charity left the Company to fill the remaining gap. It certainly did so in the case of the European mentally ill.

The Company's commercially successful days had been accompanied by penny-pinching budgets. It was well aware of the potential cost of social relief measures once the magnitude of the problem gained more visibility during the early nineteenth century. The number of European vagrants, deserters, prostitutes and the 'unemployed poor' rose steadily during the course of the early nineteenth century. In regard to Indians, the misery of the peasantry, of landless labourers and of the Indian version of the *lumpenproletariat* were increasingly manifest once British rule became firmly established. Where officials had previously assumed that a few hospitals, dispensaries, asylums and jails here and there would be enough to provide both Indians and Europeans with the 'blessings of well-regulated society', they gradually came to realize that they had miscalculated.[41] The Company consequently emphasized the limitations weighing down upon its public and health departments and whenever possible tried to shift responsibility for social welfare to the inhabitants of the various municipalities. In 1857, the court of directors emphasized that whilst local governments would be authorized to provide medicine and to meet one quarter of the maintenance cost for hospitals and dispensaries, it was the 'wealthier classes' who were 'responsible' for their establishment in the first place.[42]

There was one area for which the Company had customarily assumed responsibility: the medical care of military and naval servants. The upkeep of soldiers and sailors was strategically vital, but costly. The royal commission on the sanitary state of the army in India did not beat about the bush in its report of 1863: 'The value of a man who, with all his arms, costs the country £100 a year is considerable, and either the loss of his life, of his health, or of his efficiency, is not to be lightly regarded'.[43] The preservation of soldiers' health and fighting power was an important means of making sure that the cost of their recruitment and outfitting would be redeemed.

Atrocious as the state of the health of the soldiery in the East was during the early part of the nineteenth century (with a mortality rate for the rank and file 82 per cent higher than that for officers), there was at least some medical treatment available.[44] Once outside the tight net of the military, former soldiers were no longer entitled to any government support. Civilians could usually not count on social or medical relief, unless they constituted an immediate threat or nuisance to the European community (and hence were likely to be locked up in jail or, in the case of contagious diseases, subjected to isolation and, in later years, inoculation and vaccination). The chronically ill and those suffering from the usual range of tropical diseases, both European and Indian, typically had to fend for themselves. For sickness, the great companion of daily life in India, there was scant and substandard support in the early nineteenth century for civilians of Indian or lower-class European extraction.

The European middle-turned-ruling-class was not, despite the veneer of Georgian and Victorian humanitarianism and its fondness for institutions, particularly sensitive to the plight of the unfortunate and sick among the lower ranks of society. The Bengal General Hospital, for example, was meant for the reception of Europeans – but only those of the better classes. It would open its doors to the sick poor when an epidemic struck, but once it had passed and the authorities were sure that diseased, vagabonding Europeans would no longer endanger the community at large, admission to the institution would again be restricted. In 1835, for example, senior medical officers reminded government of the necessity to take steps to prevent municipal authorities from sending paupers to the General Hospital. This institution, they insisted, was never meant for the reception of lower-class Europeans and only extraordinary circumstances such as those of the recent plague epidemic would legitimate a diversion from the established rule.[45]

Sick Europeans of the 'lowly' kind had to make do at best with the few badly equipped premises: small local police hospitals that existed in the major cities. The clue is in the institutions' name: they were meant for the reception of the 'plebs' and received their inmates mainly from the local police who would pick up diseased paupers. However, not every sick or emaciated and destitute

European would be allowed to benefit from medicine and the attractive rations of alcohol and free meals. Typically only those were admitted who were by virtue of the nature of their disease and behaviour expected to constitute a nuisance or threat to the general public. In 1839, for example, the government of India insisted that the few pauper hospitals that existed 'must not be converted into Poor Houses or Mendicant Hospitals'.[46] Only if the hospitals had some spare funds available could the medical staff at their own discretion provide some relief 'in extreme cases'. The official aim here was clearly to cut down on government expenditure and leave responsibility for poor relief to private initiative.

The local governments' stance exemplifies the endeavour to differentiate the deserving from the undeserving poor. In so doing it echoed a crucial aspect of the English New Poor Law. Any legal equivalent to the English Poor Law was in fact lacking in the East. Yet the provincial authorities experimented with various different measures that owed much of their ideological content and practicalities to the English blueprint. Their implementation, however, was adapted to the specific circumstances of colonial rule. The provincial governments in India accepted no binding legal responsibility for the care of the sick European poor. (Nor did the government back home in England.)

However, Europeans in India were meant to be visible only as a 'formidable' ruling elite and therefore not as sick, destitute or mad. Down-and-outs and the infirm had to be kept out of sight of and separate from both well-to-do Europeans and higher-class Indians. Many of the latter had a sense of social precedence and discrimination equalled only by the more class-conscious of the British. It was this precept of colonial rule – of the maintenance of social distance between the races and between the various classes of European society – that provided the impetus for the establishment of a range of specialized institutions by provincial governments or by private subscription during a period of *laissez-faire*. It led to the cities' impressive general hospitals and the more inferior police hospitals, to the well-equipped 'higher' orphanages (for officers' and gentlemen's children) and the less welcoming 'lower' orphanages (for children of soldiers), to the treadmills, workhouses, sailors' homes, lock hospitals and lunatic asylums.

Institutionalization was just one way of making people 'invisible' who would otherwise be 'a nuisance and threat in every avenue'.[47] Another was to send them to the hills or back to England. Hill-stations in particular were thought of by medical practitioners as the ideal place for diseased Europeans to recover from the strains of military and civil duty. The climate and scenic setting were said to have resembled parts of Surrey or the Isle of Wight. However, the hills soon became the exclusive playground of well-to-do civil servants, officers and businessmen. It was not until 1864 that the government each year packed its books and pencils lock, stock and barrel and moved to the temperate surroundings of Simla. But soon after the opening of the first roads to the mountains, investment in bungalow development started. House and land prices soared as the regular exodus of British India's more prosperous classes was anticipated with the onset of the hot season. It became evident by mid-century that if any disadvantaged or sick Europeans were to be welcome in this elitist colonial refuge, it was only the man or woman with less serious afflictions, and certainly not the down-and-out or lunatic.

Only selected groups were seen as fit to benefit from the salubrious climate in the hills. Orphans were one such group, innocent enough to be tolerated. They were brought up behind closed doors, sheltered against any potentially harmful influence from the Indian environment. Similarly, convalescent soldiers would be sent to sanatoria in the hills where they were restored to their former fighting selves in rehabilitation centres well secluded from both the holidaying public and the temptations of the East. This practice was calculated to work out cheaper than the replacement of troops with new recruits from England.

In regard to other groups, such as the mentally ill and the poor, the authorities' and the public's attitude was much less favourable. The plan for a lunatic hill-station had at least been mooted, though of course not realized. But the notion that the inmates of a workhouse could possibly benefit from the climate of Simla's or Darjeeling's slopes just never came up. In the plains the location for such institutions as jails, lock-hospitals, asylums and workhouses was carefully selected. The general practice of colonial town planning provides evidence for the desire to separate the European quarters from 'native' areas and, if necessary, to demolish or move Indian markets in order to avoid their proximity to public buildings and private bungalows. It also shows that buildings such as penitentiaries were confined to the very margins of the European settlements. In the hills, a segregative public works policy could be expected to be applied even more stringently. Lower-class establishments would have offended the expatriates' sense of social distance and been contrary to the prevailing attitude towards prowlers and paupers. It was punishment rather than the impact of salubrious mountain air that was expected to work on people of that kind.

Although they were treated in very different ways, both the European destitute and the mentally ill were either to be kept securely within institutions in the plains or else deported from the colony. Sending the 'rabble' back home to England was more congenial to the social sensitivities of the European community than the establishment of asylums, workhouses and sailors' homes in India. Time-expired soldiers as well as European women of 'bad character', vagabonds and lunatics were provided with passages back to Europe, where they would be left to their own devices, or in the case of the mentally ill received into 'Pembroke House', the Company's lunatic asylum near London. Deportation was costly, but it guaranteed that social misfits and unproductive elements would be permanently out of sight and no longer a burden on the treasury.

During the earlier decades of the nineteenth century, when the Company's policy of selective immigration control was in force, the number of Europeans of the lower classes could be kept down. So could the cost of repatriation. However, the social composition of the European community in India changed considerably over the years. By the 1850s about half of the white population were 'poor Europeans'. In the face of such large numbers, repatriation was no longer economically viable, nor was the policy of immigration restriction as practicable and successful as originally planned. Deportation of those who were in possession of their wits but of not much else was consequently carried out in a less routinized way. The European community was slowly though reluctantly forced to come to terms with the fact that even under the formidable rule of the Raj there could be no European elite without the lower orders of their own kind. Those higher up the social and racial hierarchy responded by increasingly stringent social segregation and observance of rules of precedence that startled even class-conscious society in the most conservative clubs and tea-rooms in England.

The early nineteenth-century practice of repatriating those among the European mentally ill who did not recover within a year in an asylum in India certainly owed much to the Company's protectionist immigration policy and to a general and widespread antipathy towards lower-class and socially deviant people. Lunacy policy as a whole was strongly conditioned by the aspiration to discipline and control, and to make the lower strata of the European community in particular fit in with the behavioural demands seen to be appropriate to a ruling elite. It was however also the velvet glove of measures for the control and relief of Europeans in India. Unlike mendicants and vagrants, the mentally ill were not punished for their state. On the contrary, European lunatics had to be treated with 'great care and attention', whilst institutions for the poor *aimed* at providing undesirable conditions for its inmates.[48]

Conditions in the European asylum were certainly not as bad as in the workhouse and jail. This is not to say that Europeans' madness in India was perceived and treated in an unprejudiced way. The authorities were as keen to get lunatics off the cities' streets and the account books as they were to get rid of the sick and poor. Contact with the mad, or even knowledge of their presence, was not appreciated – as evidenced in the case of Lady Grey. She pressed the Bengal government to disembark a batch of lunatics from the vessel in which she was to sail home in 1833.[49] In similar vein, distinguished citizens of Madras formed a pressure group to petition government to abandon the plan to build an asylum in the midst of a recently 'gentrified' suburb. They argued that it would make the area undesirable for Europeans and lead to a fall in property prices.[50] In Bombay the authorities had the insane conveniently separated and literally 'insulated' from the general population by allocating them land on the island (later peninsula) of Salzette. The situation was similar in regard to 'native lunatic asylums'.[51]

Given a certain degree of prejudice, what made government authorities in early nineteenth-century India inclined to view the plight of the mentally ill in a somewhat less unfavourable light than that of the poor and destitute generally? Basically, they were disposed to accept mental illness as an unfortunate mishap rather than the result of malice, self-inflicted misfortune, or fecklessness. During this period, madness was widely seen in European countries to be 'a calamity the heaviest which can well befall a rational and responsible being'.[52] Ever since Philippe Pinel's release of the mad in the Bicetre of Paris from their chains and shackles, in the late eighteenth century, humane treatment and avoidance of mechanical restraint had emerged as the most enlightened response to mental derangement.

The less censorious attitude towards the mentally ill resulted to a large extent from the fact that madness unlike destitution crossed barriers of social class. It was true that great fortunes could be as easily lost in the East as they were at times gained. But rarely would a gentleman fall victim to destitution and end up in the city's gutters. Madness in contrast could reduce any bright officer's or government servant's intelligent conversation to inchoate babble. From their opening, lunatic asylums in India had been occupied by inmates of all social classes. As a consequence, the authorities did not measure lunacy against the same yardstick of culpability as destitution and mendicancy. The presence of higher-class patients in the provincial asylums therefore ensured that the asylum sector – despite its function within colonial society as a whole of ensuring peace and order – would not be intrinsically linked with a penal policy for paupers. The mentally ill were not criminalized as was the case with Indian tribal communities from the 1840s, for example.

The preferential treatment of European in contrast to Indian lunatics was however not beyond criticism. Since government had made asylums open their doors and accounts to regular inspection, critics had voiced their disapproval of what they considered to be highly exaggerated provision for the mentally ill. Inmates were downgraded from first to second class and wealthy relatives asked to pay for their maintenance in the asylum. Criticism focused mainly on the high cost of asylum provision. The more general question of whether local governments in India ought to be responsible at all for the maintenance of European lunatics there and on arrival back home in England was not confronted until 1852. Then the sympathetic policy towards the European mentally ill came as close as it ever did to being queried in principle. By that time the three asylums for Europeans in India were hopelessly overcrowded.

Conditions had deteriorated because of the lack of funds available for staffing, refurbishment and reconstruction, and a reorganization of the civil administration's medical department was under way.

The principle of segregating the mad from other social groups, such as the sick, the poor and the destitute, and treating them in a comparatively favourable way was under scrutiny. The still broader question was raised why government should do more 'for insane East Indians, or other Christians, or people of European habits, than it does for its Native Hindoo and Mahomedan subjects when in the same lamentable condition'.[53] The exception or 'the only speciality', it was argued by Bengal government officials, were Europeans and in particular 'those of the lower ranks' and in government employ. They should as hitherto be maintained out of public funds. However, whilst the authorities acknowledged a moral duty to provide for the mentally ill, they were under no legal obligation to do so. Hence, Lord Dalhousie, who presided over the Bengal council chambers between 1848 and 1856, had the medical service reorganized in 1856 and put lunatic asylums on an administrative footing similar to that of county asylums in England – except that the institutions for Europeans had to make separate arrangements for first-class patients. The period of sporadic measures and relatively sympathetic government policies had come to an end. The sterner spirit of centrally administered public institutions and of clearly circumscribed regulations superseded asylums' hitherto more permissive arrangements.

Administrative Reforms and Legal Provision

Lord Dalhousie's reforms certainly initiated a period of significant change in policy towards the insane in India. It was considered long overdue. In Bengal the medical authorities had already in the 1830s advocated a change in the asylum's system of management. They wanted the then privately owned facility to be taken over by government and the medical board to be vested with the exclusive authority to manage and control institutional affairs. Further, improvements in asylum conditions had been suggested in Madras and Bombay since the number of institutionalized lunatics there had increased significantly from about the late 1830s and early 1840s onwards. In both places the attempted amelioration of overcrowding by regular extensions and other patching-up efforts was no longer sufficient. The situation in the 'native lunatic asylums' had become no less pressing.[54]

On the grounds of numbers alone then, lunacy provision had necessarily gained a higher profile in the treasury's accounts and was increasingly liable to government scrutiny. Yet neither the Company's court of directors nor the provincial governments in India considered an extension of European and Indian asylums and the concomitant increase in funds to be feasible. On the contrary. The authorities were determined to cut down on the expense of the ever-growing 'general department' under which medical and social welfare matter were subsumed. Leaving conditions to deteriorate further was however no longer a viable solution, as consequential effects from select committees preceding the passing of the trend-setting lunacy acts of 1842 and 1845 in England were already in the offing. The European public could soon be expected to turn their attention to the plight of the Indian insane in particular and to what might well be interpreted as conditions very much inferior to those existing in England.

In fact a Dr G. A. Berwick offered in 1847 his services to the Bengal government in an attempt to improve mental institutions in India and to put them on a footing comparable to what he had seen in the more advanced amongst British asylums. His suggestion contained however not only what the province's medical board called 'the crude and incongruous scheme of assembling Europeans and Natives in one Establishment' for the sake of better surveillance (which was anathema to the Europeans in India as much as to the Hindu and Muslim community), but of making ample provision for the Indian insane, the number of which he anticipated to rise (which was contrary to the authorities' austere financial policy).[55] Berwick's plan was consequently shelved.

Nevertheless, public opinion was in the process of changing – shifting from the early enthusiasm of a Sir Andrew Halliday who considered asylums in India as superior to English institutions to the more gloomy picture of colonial institutions as dank 'dungeons' towards the middle of the century. In Bombay the asylum superintendent had to firmly refute allegations in 1852 by an anonymous writer in one of the town's newsletters that the asylum was a 'disgrace to the British government and name'.[56] And in 1854 Dr J. Macpherson complained that 'the Asylums now in existence in India…have, some of them at least, all the appearance of jails'.[57] This significant change of opinion on the state of India's asylums certainly owed much to earlier naive overstatement and the ambition to play off policy makers and philanthropists in the British Isles against the Company's administrators in order to speed up reforms. It is however also indicative of an actual worsening of asylum conditions in India because of the governments' restrictions on public spending in a period of continual increase in patients' numbers. As governor Falkland expressed it: 'under the present financial embarrassment before we can attend to the dictates of humanity it becomes our duty to provide for the security of the people'.[58]

What then *were* the options open to the Company and the executive governments in India in the 1850s? They could either maintain the status quo (thereby risking accusations of neglect and mismanagement), or extend existing provision (bringing on the auditor-general's disapproval), or else they could re-organize the whole system from its roots. The latter was exactly what was achieved during Dalhousie's term of office and the remaining two years before the Company ceased to be in charge of the administration of British India. To begin with, the private trade in lunacy and consequently the potential for financial extravagance and corruption that persisted in Bengal until 1856 was done away with and government took over the management of the province's lunatics. At the same time any significant future increase in the cost of asylum provision arising from an increase in the number of inmates was pre-empted by a drastic reduction in all but first-class patients' maintenance rates. And last but not least the decision-making process was considerably simplified and the potential for friction among government servants reduced by investing a single superintending surgeon with the control of each province's medical institutions.

Most significantly, however, a package of new laws was devised that aimed at unifying lunacy provision in India and at integrating English and Indian regulations. The Indian Lunatic Asylum Act was one of three acts passed by the legislative council of India in 1858 with the explicit aim of bringing the legal situation in India in line with that in England and Wales. It provided a uniform legal basis for the establishment of public lunatic asylums by the executive governments of each province and aimed at preventing one of the threats most dreaded by the Victorians: wrongful confinement. At the same time it allowed for the maintenance within public institutions of lunatics who were neglected or treated cruelly by their relatives or friends. The act's main purpose was certainly (like its English model) to facilitate the growth of publicly funded and controlled asylums in place of privately owned institutions – an important step in that it accorded well with the general tendency towards the consolidation and centralization of the colonial state. Special concessions were however made to Indian circumstances. The most important was that the erection of asylums was made optional rather than compulsory. In so doing the act reflected the authorities' general conviction that whilst intervention by the colonial state in civil affairs was seen as necessary, the high maintenance costs of public institutions were considered a drain on state revenue and the specifics and idiosyncrasies of colonial administration in the various parts of British India were expected to impede any imposition of uniform requirements.

The Indian Lunatic Asylum Act also empowered the executive governments to grant licences for private asylums. This provision may at first sight appear contrary to the tendency in England and the very intent of the act to restrict the private 'trade in lunacy' in favour of public institutions. Previous experience in Bengal, too, had shown that confinement of public patients in a private asylum was bound to lead to sometimes irreconcilable conflict between proprietor and medical authorities. The key to the act's seemingly incongruent provision lies with the fact that both in England and India public institutions possessed an ambivalent image. Persons of all ranks and walks of life were to be admitted into public asylums. In the language of the law this meant that 'every darogah or district police officer' had to send to the magistrate 'all persons found wandering at large…who are deemed to be lunatics, and all persons believed to be dangerous by reason of lunacy'.[59] What in fact the Indian act provided for was the possibility of two separate types of institution: one (public) for paupers and lower-class people, and one (private) for upper class lunatics. In so doing it reflected (if only as an option) the tendency of English developments in consequence of the passing of the Lunatics Act – namely the retention of private houses for the rich.

The acts of 1858 contained provisions that had in England been considered as most controversial. The concern about the prevention of wrongful confinement and the preservation of individual freedom, for example, which had been occasioned by the concomitant demand for the state to evolve an interventionist stance, had been a typical matter of contention for many decades. Despite this, the discussion preceding the passing of the Indian acts was short and uncontroversial. After all, recourse was had to laws that had already been enforced in England and were at the time of their application in India considered to be sufficiently comprehensive and humanitarian.[60] At the same time the new regulations were open to interpretation within the various contexts in which administrators found themselves. With the enactments of 1858 (which were in slightly amended forms to be in force until 1912), the period of patchy legal provision and considerable variety of approaches towards the management of the mad came to an end. From this time on one can speak of a 'system' of asylum provision in British India. What the law provided for was basically a system that was structurally akin to that extant in the British Isles, adaptable to Indian circumstances.

Prior to the momentous enactments of 1858, legal provision had been made in 1849 and 1851 for a special group among the insane – 'criminal' lunatics: those amongst the mentally ill who had committed a violent act that would under ordinary circumstances have been punishable under the penal law. The association between states of 'unsoundness of mind' and the law was not peculiar to colonial rule alone, nor was it typical only of Anglo-Saxon legislation. Irrespective of the state of the law, 'criminal lunatics' had been subject to greater public apprehension than the mentally ill in general. This was not only due to the often reasonable fear that they might repeat a violent action, but also because it was frequently in question whether a verdict of 'unsoundness of mind' was legitimate. Shamming was after all suspected to be common practice among military servants. Insanity in particular was feigned as a last recourse by soldiers tired of military duty in the East and unable to buy themselves out of the service. The common view was that lunatics could not be held responsible for their actions and that they should be released once their mental derangement had subsided. From 1849 onwards, and even more so from 1851 when the legal situation was clearly circumscribed, early discharge would however no longer be guaranteed, as criminal lunatics had to be transferred to the jail in order to serve the full sentence in case they recovered from the mental affliction prior to the end of their term.

There were however quite a few cases, particularly in the military and navy in which a verdict of 'unsoundness of mind' was considered (mistakenly or not) a softer option than the usual disciplinary punishment for insubordination, desertion, or violence. The first half of the nineteenth century was after all the period when discipline among European troops and sailors was frequently enforced by means of the loathed cat-o'-nine-tails and by execution. 'I saw so many flogged', wrote a grenadier after about a decade's service in the East, 'that I was heartily tired of soldiering'.[61] Witnessing within one month the execution of a comrade who had been found guilty of 'striking the Surgeon...with his shut fist' and of two others from similar offences, he concluded that 'such scenes...only tend to make the soldier loathe instead of honouring his profession'.

Being declared insane was also perceived by some desperate to see the last of soldiering as a way out of life-long military service that was only reduced to between seven and 21 years during times of war in order to attract a greater number of recruits. Service in the Victorian army was generally acknowledged to be an extremely stressful trade. The recommendation, published in *The Times* in 1858, that 'if a man is anxious to get rid of his life without having recourse to measures of direct suicide, the most honourable way to obtain this desirable end is to enter as a private' in a British regiment, was a sarcastic expression of this. Given the insalubrious aspects of military life, lunacy appealed to quite a few as an alternative to the madness of service in the East. Not only simple soldiers or sailors resorted to working their ticket in this way. Officers, too, sometimes made the most of the law's insanity clause.

The verdict of 'unsoundness of mind' and its medico-legal implications had in England been subject to controversy throughout the century. Similarly, when the legislative council of India was in the process of framing the new 1849 act aimed at integrating English with Indian rules and in particular ensuring that a defendant could no longer 'on a Medical Officer's opinion differing from that recorded on the trial be let loose on society', arguments against the insanity clause were advanced.[62] Drinkwater Bethune, the president of the Indian law commission, for example, believed that the plea of lunacy should be disallowed and that it should be left to the 'prerogative of mercy' to pardon those few 'unhappy persons' who were really free from guilt. He was against framing the law in India in accordance with English law as he considered the latter in its practical application 'far from being in a clear and satisfactory state'.

To make his point, Bethune cited the anecdote of the 'notorious Jonathan Martin' who had set fire to York Cathedral, suggesting that the plea of insanity was then widely discussed by patients in the asylums and that the saying was much in their mouths 'You know they cannot hang him for he is mad'.[63] Basically his Honour considered English law to be too 'tender', pointing at 'the shocking acquittals which have been multiplied lately in England'. He believed that it was preferable by far to deter people from giving 'free vent to their passions' than doing justice to what he considered to be a merely theoretical legal objection: the alleged danger of making those very few who were not able to control their actions accountable for them. In this he was supported by Lord Dalhousie, who shared the opinion that the plea of insanity served in the majority of cases those who knew that they would from their supposed or actual lunacy escape punishment. The governor-general succinctly summarized his point: 'As long as he knows he is doing a wrong, no matter whether he is urged to do it by [diseased] workings of his brain or not, he should in my opinion suffer the penalty of that wrong.'[64]

Despite such strong objection at the highest level of government in India, provisions for the criminal insane were finally made. The draft act was (with but few formal changes) assented to by the governor-general in December 1848. Both he and the law commissioner were very well aware that although criminal lunacy constituted a difficult medico-legal problem, their view on this matter was not consistent with 'general opinion' in England and would therefore be 'shared by very few'.[65] Bethune rightly assumed that even if deterrent regulations were passed by the council in India (which he very much doubted), they would be vetoed by the Company's court of director in England. What is more, it was not considered right that, as Dalhousie put it, the local government should legislate 'in principles which are so much beyond the present standard of the law at home'.[66] To that judgement Bethune could not but agree, as he also maintained – albeit less successfully – in regard to the Indian penal code in general a rather orthodox position that closely followed English enactments. And last but not least lunacy provision had not a high enough profile for government in India to induce authorities such as the law commissioner and the governor general to go against 'general opinion' in pursuit of measures they would personally have preferred.

Though Bethune and Dalhousie considered the criminal lunatics law as too 'tender', the practical consequences for the insane themselves were anything but a reason for rejoicing. Together with Dalhousie's other reforms of the asylum sector, the criminal lunacy legislation helped to enforce a strict system of segregation and discrimination. Criminal lunatics were kept separate from other asylum inmates and were not usually allowed to partake in the few amusements and privileges granted to them. It is true that the verdict of 'not guilty on account of unsoundness of mind' could be abused. Conversely, the fate of a person who was detained for life in the asylum or jail 'even though there be a restoration to reason' could by the standards of neither liberal nor conservative opinion really be considered fortunate when the ever more parsimonious institutional conditions that were enforced towards the middle of the century for all but first-class patients are taken into account.

The enactments of 1849 and 1851 were considered by district judges in India to be most important milestones in the consolidation of an hitherto open legal situation. With the act of 1849 the authority in the criminal courts necessary for the detention of persons who had been acquitted on grounds of insanity had been established. Until that date the 'prevention of danger to the community' could not be ensured, as criminal courts had not been vested with legal authority to attach any conditions to the liberation of a person who had been found *non compos mentis*. The more comprehensive regulation came however into force in 1851. The Criminal Lunatics Act gave authorities other than those who had passed the original verdict the power to keep a criminal lunatic confined. Thus a person who had been tried by, say, the Bengal court and was subsequently transferred to Bombay, could be kept in detention. The act also guaranteed that criminal lunatics of European descent would not accumulate in institutions in India, but would instead be sent to England. There they were received into jails (and from 1863 into the State Criminal Asylum at Broadmoor) rather than

Figure 3. Mare Street, Hackney. View looking north, showing Pembroke House Lunatic Asylum, the surgeon's house to the south, on the corner of Helmsley Street, part of the wall of Mare Street Baptist Church, and the shops to the north of Pembroke House, 1871.

Pembroke House, where the Company's lunatics would under ordinary circumstances be accommodated.[67]

The consequences of the Criminal Lunatics Acts were not only of a long-term medico-legal but also of a short-term practical nature. By the 1840s the European asylums in the three main centres were sufficiently overcrowded to make any increase in admission rates (as was to be expected as a direct result of the new legislation) the last straw that would threaten the institutions' capacity to cope. As no funds for the extension of asylum provision had been allocated by the provincial governments, a more restrictive admission policy appeared to be the only way of dealing with the growth in patient numbers. The problem was most pressing in regard to the various 'native lunatic asylums' and in Bombay and Madras where, unlike in Calcutta, Europeans and Eurasians were admitted alongside Indians. The question was who among the insane should in future be excluded? If criminal lunatics had by force of the law to be admitted, it was other inmates who had to go. Priorities had to be set and the obvious choice was to prevent local authorities from certifying those among the Indian insane who were considered 'harmless' or merely 'idiotic'.

The basic criterion for the admission of Indians was to become their danger to the community at large rather than their state of mind. The criminal lunacy laws therefore did much to bring out into the open one major aspect inherent in lunacy policy towards Indians, namely its double function as a means of guaranteeing public peace and order, and of controlling and disciplining socially harmful misfits. The oft-proclaimed humanitarian ambition of governments in India to provide a refuge or retreat for those amongst its subjects who were afflicted by insanity and idiocy (regardless of whether they be violent) had fallen prey to the necessities of cost-effective institutional management and considerations for the safety of the public and particularly the expatriate community. Dr J. Macpherson, temporarily in charge of the Calcutta Asylum, could thus pointedly summarize the Indian governments' lunacy policy by contrasting the situation in England where 'we provide for our poor, for our sick, and for our insane' with that in India where 'we exhibit an utter disregard of all except criminal lunatics'.[68]

In the case of European lunatics the situation was somewhat different though as both the violent and the harmless amongst them were to be regarded as fit subjects for institutionalization and subsequent transfer to England. This does not mean that the authorities were guided only by the ambition to provide, if not for Indians', then at least for Europeans' 'reception and treatment on the most approved system' (although officials such as governor Falkland may genuinely have interpreted their office to be that of an agent for humanitarian measures).[69] Nor could the tendency amongst the British to 'cling together' and to support their fellow expatriates on patriotic grounds sufficiently account for the preferential confinement of Europeans of all sorts. Patriotism and a sense of togetherness could after all easily be undermined by observance of rules of social precedence, feelings of social superiority and the omnipresent Victorian aspiration to show kindness only to those who were seen to be 'deserving'. A large proportion of the insane were in fact lower-class soldiers. (In 1850, the Bengal asylum for example confined 55 patients of 'European habits', of whom 33 or 60 per cent were in the second class. In Bombay, in 1851/52, 12 out of a total of 15 Europeans belonged to the lower classes, with all but one, a female pauper, having previously served in the army and navy.[70])

If humanitarian and patriotic grounds alone could not easily account for the policy of attaching no conditions to Europeans' admission to the asylum, and in particular for the neglect of the (at other times) so decisive factor of social background, what then were the reasons behind it? To a large extent it was authorities' endeavour to leave no white person at large whose behaviour could endanger public safety or military discipline, or which could be considered to adversely affect the prestige of the European community by exhibiting uncontrollably irrational or indecent behaviour unbecoming to a ruling elite. Moreover, in the face of overcrowded institutions and financial pressures, European lunatics were not the prime target for admission restrictions and cost-cutting exercises. Compared with the steadily growing number of institutionalized Eurasian and Indian lunatics, the number of Europeans in institutions in India was negligible. This was of course largely due to the established practice of sending them back to Europe at regular intervals – towards the middle of the century as often as twice a year. European lunacy consequently became less and less visible both within and without institutions in India. The European mentally ill could therefore not possibly be perceived to be the cause of crowding in institutions in India and even if the Company had been alarmed by the high cost of repatriating Europeans certified insane, it would not have been inclined to support a policy that would have made European lunatics objects for public comment because of their visible presence in the community.

It appears then that the consolidation of lunacy policy in the three provinces and the legal provisions for British India's European mentally ill had been effected towards the end of the Company's administration of East Indian affairs despite sometimes conflicting ideological aspirations. Measures were executed by a local administration not always free from corruption yet always with one eye on public opinion in both England and India as to the appropriate treatment of the sick, the poor and the mad in a colonial context that demanded racial and social segregation, economy of public expenditure and the separation of violent lunatics from the socially harmless insane.

Chapter 3

THE INSTITUTIONS

The Role of Institutionalization

When, in 1858, the Crown took over the political administration of British India, it was also to take charge of public institutions previously established by the East India Company. The Company's legacy of jails, penitentiaries, hospitals and dispensaries (and to a lesser extent of orphanages, workhouses and schools) was impressive. There existed also several lunatic asylums. The provinces of Bengal, Bombay and Madras each boasted an asylum for the reception of Europeans, whilst nearly every district had its own 'native lunatic asylum'. Further institutions for the mentally ill had been established in more recently annexed areas, such as Burma, the Punjab and Sind, as well as in the coastal centre of Sri Lanka and in such remote territorial acquisitions as Penang and Singapore. In addition to these specialized receptacles, lunatics 'up-country' in inaccessible and desolate areas could be locked up for shorter periods in the more ubiquitous local jails and in cells adjoining dispensaries and regimental hospitals. The British Empire of the nineteenth century was thus, it would appear, well provided with institutions for the confinement of deranged Europeans and Asians.

The Company's provision for European lunatics extended back into the colonial motherland itself. In England, Pembroke House, a privately managed madhouse, specialized in the treatment of insane Europeans sent home from India by the East India Company. This was not the only institution in England for returned lunatics. Distinguished places such as Ticehurst Asylum also received many a mad officer and gentleman or lady whose fortunes allowed for confinement in style, whilst Haslar and Great Yarmouth Hospitals as well as Chatham Asylum had provision for insane military and naval servants who had (as in the case of royal army servants for example) not been deemed eligible for maintenance in Pembroke House at the East India Company's expense. At the bottom end of the social scale, guardians of the poor in sea ports where East Indiamen put ashore reluctantly made provision in public asylums or workhouses for pauper lunatics found wandering at large subsequent to their arrival from India and for those who had an eventual relapse after temporary spontaneous recovery on board ship.

Provision for the mentally ill on such an organized scale may legitimately be regarded as an institutional 'network'. The web of Victorian institutionalism, it would appear, closed in on mad Europeans and colonial subjects in the East alike – from Lahore to Colombo and from Bombay to the Straits and back to London. However, the numbers involved were small – still nowhere near those characteristic of 'the great confinement' of Western Europe and of France in particular. The European lunatic asylum in Calcutta contained in the late 1850s around 100 Europeans, whilst those in Bombay and Madras provided on average for not more than ten Europeans each.[1] The small number of European patients is of course partly a result of the Company's policy of repatriating its insane at least once a year. However, Pembroke House, the major institution for the confinement of 'Indian Insanes' – as returned mental patients of European parentage were called in England – did not see an extraordinary number of patients pass through its premises either. From its opening in 1818 until the changeover to the Crown in 1858 about 500 lunatics with previous Indian experience had been on this institution's books.[2] Even if one would allow for roughly as many mental patients again ending up (rightly or wrongly) in one of England's military, pauper and private asylums and for deaths during the arduous and lengthy sea journey round the Cape of Good Hope, the total number of Europeans certified 'mad' and confined in a mental institution of one kind or another on arrival from India was not particularly remarkable.

A similar picture prevailed in regard to non-European asylum inmates in British India. Although the absolute numbers involved here may sound more substantial (with the seven 'native lunatic asylums' in Bengal and the North-Western Provinces for example confining in 1854 between 52 and 189 patients, bringing the total to a little over 1,000) they were by no means proportional to these provinces' overall population figures.[3] Despite further provision for lunatics in small stations' jails, only a 'small proportion' of the Indian mentally ill were institutionalized – as had been revealed during the extended investigation into the state of 'native lunatic asylums' from 1852 to 1854.

Institutional statistics of course are never indicative of the actual incidence of 'mental illness' – even if there was no problem in defining what precisely was to be understood by such a complicated social construct. Nor, for that matter, do numbers by themselves reveal the importance attributed to the institutional treatment of the insane. However, institutional statistics, if contrasted with the estimated number of persons at large considered mentally ill, can reveal the frequency with which recourse is taken by the state to the institutionalization of a certain proportion of the people considered insane.

In the case of British India any attempt to arrive at even an approximate assessment of the number of the mentally ill (inside and outside various institutional settings) is fraught with particular problems. Take again the case of the Indian insane. Government officials as well as medical practitioners considered the number of confined lunatics to be but a small fraction of the total. Surgeon J. Macpherson was even led to assert sarcastically in 1854 that

> in India…we rejoice to say, that we have no complaint to make of institutions mismanaged, that we have no heart-rending records to shew of cruelty towards the insane, or of any of those abuses which formerly gave rise to the deepest indignation in England.[4]

This was so, Macpherson argued, because only scant institutional provision for the confinement of India's mentally ill existed: 'Our grievances here assume quite another shape…. we have in India to lament the almost entire absence of Asylums of any sort of description'. Governor Falkland had in 1850 similarly bemoaned the insufficiency of public provision for those amongst the insane in Bombay who, though harmless, were in the governor's judgement still entitled to 'sympathy and assistance from [their] fellow men'.[5] There had also been frequent complaints by European citizens, greatly stirred by reports of madmen allegedly waylaying nervous gentlemen in dark and spooky hollows. The Company had as yet clearly failed to securely lock up many a potentially threatening lunatic.

Although government officials, medical practitioners and European citizens agreed that institutional provision for Indian lunatics was inadequate, their concerted lamentation was apparently insufficient to induce the Company to allocate more funds for the amelioration of the situation. More importantly in this context, although the numerical insufficiency of asylums had been condemned, nobody could as yet provide exact data on the relative incidence of madness amongst Indians, nor could anybody estimate with even a moderate degree of reliability the number of lunatics at large. Attempts at estimates were hopelessly contradictory, being based mainly on guesswork and speculation. The superintendent of police in Bombay, for example, who was in 1849 entrusted with establishing reliable population figures, admitted failure.[6] Even census officials in the 1870s pointed out that information on 'lunatics' and 'idiots' was difficult to obtain because of families' tendency to hide deranged relatives from public sight, on the one hand, and the enumerators' lack of diagnostic skill, on the other. Data on the number of the mentally ill (as on the population as a whole) could not, it was suggested, 'be accepted as of much value'.[7]

The situation was no better in regard to European lunatics. Here institutional provision had never been considered quite so inadequate. On the contrary, space was always available for European lunatics in any one of the three main receptacles. To ensure this, Eurasian and Indian patients were made to vacate rooms and squeeze into overcrowded wards (in Bombay) and

Europeans of higher social standing were boarded out to more 'suitable' premises (in Madras) towards the middle of the century when the building had become dilapidated. Nevertheless, the incidence of mental illness amongst Europeans cannot easily be deduced from the asylums' statistics alone. It was difficult to delineate mental illness from physical disease or social delinquency. It was a fairly arbitrary decision whether a debilitated, perhaps violent or petulant, hungry vagrant, suffering from some disease, was a fit subject for reception – if at all – into the madhouse, the jail, the hospital, the sailor's home, or the house of correction. The lines between disease, crime, insanity and poverty could rarely be clearly drawn. It is also difficult to establish the frequency with which mentally deranged Europeans were dealt with by means other than confinement in one of the provincial mental hospitals. Apart from the asylums in Calcutta, Madras and Bombay, private lunatic asylums received Europeans of a 'respectable class' and civil surgeons made separate provision for private patients. Yet no data are available that

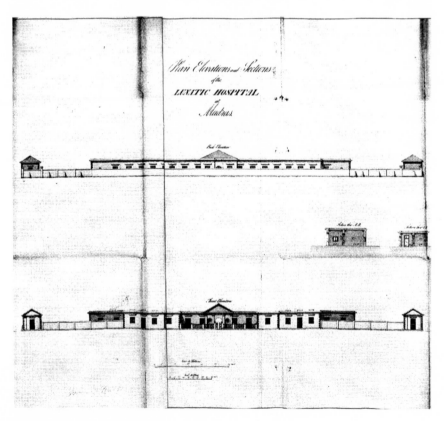

Figure 4. Lunatic Asylum, Madras, 1852 (plan elevations and sections).

could indicate the frequency with which recourse was had to facilities in the private sector. Further, a number of insane civilians simply remained in the care of their friends and relations, as the Bengal medical board pointed out in 1851: 'from natural affection and also from disinclination to lodge their relatives in a public Mad House, however well conducted, the patients are retained by their families'.[8]

Moreover, unruly and strange behaviour exhibited by personnel in the naval and military services was met in the first instance by disciplinary action such as incarceration, flogging and physical training rather than specialized medical care. Only the most serious cases of mental derangement and alleged 'feigned madness' were registered in regimental statistics. Casualty and suicide rates, too, were often driven by mental problems – yet such connections cannot easily be deduced from the statistics. Finally, only a small number of those diagnosed by the military as insane were eventually despatched with the invalids of the season from military camps in the interior to asylums in the provincial capitals.[9] Junior and senior officers were often sent straight to the nearest port of embarkation for transfer back to England. Lieutenant K. B., for example, had been diagnosed 'intellectually insane' and kept under observation at the 1st Grenadiers' camp for about three months before he was deported without ever being admitted to a lunatic asylum in India.[10] Soldiers and sailors, too, would (contrary to the officially prescribed procedure) not always be received into the asylum. Surgeon Macpherson noted in 1854 that

> about one European soldier has annually passed through the [Calcutta] Asylum, and probably nine more may have gone home with the invalids, not being considered bad enough cases to be sent to the Asylum, or may have been sent with invalids, via Bombay, or may have died in the acute stage.[11]

Macpherson based the estimate on his experience as army surgeon and asylum superintendent. He finally arrived, on the basis of his own calculations, at a number 'absolutely sent away from their Regiments for insanity' of 8.5 per 1,000 (for the period 1848 to 1851). He noted that 'the number of admissions into Hospital for insanity among European Troops in Bengal for the four years ending with 1851–52 has been 2.7 per thousand'.[12] Other sources, too, indicate that the incidence of lunacy amongst Europeans may have been a multiple of what official asylum figures lead one to believe. Regimental statistics drawn up for the commission on the state of the health of the army in India reveal that in the Bengal Infantry, for example, 97 per cent of those affected with mental derangement during the period 1847 to 1851 were reported to have returned to duty again. Personnel suffering from insanity were admitted to the regimental hospital without ever being transferred to the province's only specialist institution, consequently not appearing in asylum statistics.[13]

Two points of importance emerge from reflection on the statistics of institutionalization. First, the lunatic asylum was of but minor numerical significance compared with both confinement in less specialized institutions, such as hospitals and jails, and informal, disciplinary or private methods of dealing with unruly and unreasonable behaviour. Second, available statistics provide evidence only for inner-institutional trends and the demographic characteristics of inmates: for fluctuations in admission numbers and mortality rates, patients' professional background and the diagnoses made, the comparative numbers of first- and of second-class patients, of males and females, and the diet and medical intervention prescribed for different groups. No generalized statement about the incidence of mental illness amongst Europeans in India can be deduced from these data, nor can the socio-political and symbolic relevance of mental institutions within the context of British colonial rule be assessed on the basis of asylum statistics and institutional policy alone. If we want to know more about why, initially, only moderate recourse was taken to confinement in specialized institutions and what the role of the lunatic asylum was considered to be within the fabric of British colonial rule, we will have to turn to evidence other than that produced in the institutions themselves.

The arguments employed by government officials in favour of the establishment of new asylums in various provinces under British rule are particularly revealing. They were always the same. The establishment of 'native lunatic asylums' in Bengal had in 1806, for example, been sanctioned even by the Company's ever cost-conscious court of directors – despite an earlier decree that no large outlay of public funds could be allowed 'at a time when the Finances of the Company experience[d] the pressure of one very expensive War recently concluded, and another lately commenced'.[14] The asylums, the court proclaimed, had 'undoubtedly' for their object 'the protection of the Public on the one hand, and the relief of the most unhappy Class of human beings on the other'. Despite financial stringency, humanitarian considerations as well as concerns for public peace and order made the court 'by no means disposed either to pronounce any harsh or rigid strictures'.

The asylum for Europeans in Calcutta, too, had in 1802 been approved on a similar understanding. The erection of the Madras Lunatic Asylum in 1793/4 had been sanctioned by the authorities in England and India because of the great advantage anticipated to accrue to the town population and to future patients. The hospital board had recommended the asylum project, pointing out 'how beneficial the adoption of it would be to the Community at large by affording Security against the perpetration of those Acts of Violence which had been so frequently Committed by unrestrained Lunatics'.[15]

The cost of such benevolent control impacted heavily on the Company's revenue. Despite authorities' endeavours to economize on other public services, provincial governments seemed prepared to disburse significant sums for its peace of mind and that of its citizens. The rent paid over a 50 year period by the Madras government, for example, had been an exorbitant three and a half *lakh* of rupees (Rs 350,000). The rate of maintenance in the lunatic asylum had been double that of the general hospital.[16] In other provinces, too, asylum provision cost the Company many times what it took to maintain institutions of comparable standard in England. Maintenance costs in hospitals and, more so, in jails were far below those of madhouses.

Madhouse-owners undoubtedly overcharged the provincial governments. They kept as many inmates as possible at first-class rates on which the profit margin was wider. Particularly in Bengal during the earlier decade of the century, rates had been charged that, in the words of the medical board in 1847, were

> on a scale of liberality to all connected with the Institution which those accustomed to the more exact and healthier administration of the Public resources of the present day can scarcely contemplate without astonishment.[17]

For example, Miss F., who had as an 'out door ward of Kidderpoor school' previously earned Rs 35 per month, was maintained on the rate of Rs 100 per month in the asylum. This made available to her 'the enjoyment of a degree of ease and luxury, that [she] never could have expected to procure for [herself] in health' and which, it was speculated by the medical board, must for her as much as for many others with her 'at first have been irksome…from its very novelty'.[18] The fact that many of the patients who benefited from such 'extravagance' were of mixed race, had by the middle of the century undoubtedly become the major cause for concern.[19] But, for poor Europeans and lower-class military personnel, treatment on a preferential scale was seen to be no less 'irksome' and the maintenance rate for them was finally also curtailed. Despite cuts in rates, the Calcutta asylum (which had been in the hands of the Beardsmore family for nearly four decades) was in 1850 still likened to 'Spence's', the town's luxury hotel: the Beardsmores' charges, the accountant general pondered, 'are the same as Spence's; but there it's to be feared the comparison ends'.[20]

In fairness to the Beardsmores and other asylum proprietors, it must be conceded that the high cost of asylum provision was only partly caused by their tendency to overcharge. Even after Lord Dalhousie's reorganization of the medical service and lunatic asylum sector in the 1850s, the expense of the European insane was still considerably above average costs in England.

House prices in the three main provinces were notoriously high and construction and re-construction of asylum buildings was no less costly. Then there was the relatively higher cost involved in keeping inmates of 'European habits' in accordance with the comfort and standards to which they had come to be accustomed and obliged to live up to in the colony. In addition to nurses or 'keepers', personal servants were employed to cater for patients' special whims and some additional European staff had to be available in case a patient needed to be put under restraint and would have felt humiliated to be held down by a 'native' keeper. Such special personnel requirements made heavy demands on the asylums' already hard-pressed finances.

Nevertheless, the Company seemed reluctant to do without the particular convenience that a madhouse was seen to constitute. What was it then that made this costly institution catering for but a small proportion of the insane so desirable? The preservation of public peace and order was certainly a main object of concern to Company officials. However, despite the urgency that seems to be conveyed in official statements, the number of institutionalized lunatics at the turn of the century, when most institutions in India had been set up, was even lower than towards the middle of the nineteenth century. The asylum in Bengal confined in 1818 only 30 European and Eurasian patients who, it might well be argued, could not *in toto* possibly have constituted any insuperable threat to citizens' peace in a place as bustling and unruly as Calcutta. Similarly, Bombay had (in around 1800) only three and Madras (in 1808) 21 Europeans locked up – numbers that make the talk of the places' 'absolute necessity' appear somewhat exaggerated.

Just as the maintenance of public order cannot entirely justify the expenditure on asylums in India, neither can humanitarian motives alone. According to contemporary reformist ideology, humanitarian considerations and altruism were not incompatible with individual self-interest and the Company's wish to control, regulate and even subjugate people who were considered to exhibit socially undesirable behaviour. Humanitarian considerations, too, had their limits as is evidenced by the decision in the late 1840s to exclude the intellectually disabled from institutionalization on the basis of the relative unobtrusiveness and social harmlessness of their symptoms. Had humanitarian considerations been the main impetus behind the upkeep of highly expensive institutions, then the local governments would indeed not, as governor Falkland succinctly pointed out in 1849, have considered 'to debar a friendless lunatic from all professional aid merely because he may be quite inoffensive'.[21]

The European lunatic asylum in British India possessed a more complex role that went beyond the hackneyed rhetoric of sound order and humanitarian aspiration. It was, along with other public institutions such as the hospital and jail, one of the symbolic markers of European superiority. When, for example,

Lord Auckland in his capacity as governor-general toured the Upper Provinces from 1837 to 1840, he never missed the opportunity to visit the commercial, police and medical establishments of even the smallest of British stations. On 28 November 1837 he travelled to Mirzapur and after being greeted by 'the usual assortment of magistrates, judges, collectors, &c. &c.' he immediately 'went off' to see the jail and the famous local carpet manufactories.[22] A week later, in Allahabad, he went to the 'native schools and jails'. In Kanpur, a couple of weeks later, he and 'the gentlemen' of his entourage 'went to the prison to see some Thugs'. Encamped near Moradabad, a 'cheerful-looking station' (though one where his Excellency's sister, Emily Eden, was not able to 'find anything to sketch'), he was in the position to pass some time by visiting the local jail after the 'durbar' put on for local officials.

Manufactories, schools, dispensaries, hospitals, court rooms and jails were some of the showpieces of Western colonialism at work in India – brick-and-mortar manifestations of British patriotic pride and self-satisfaction intended to inspire the awe of the indigenous population. According to contemporary understanding the very existence of institutions was one of *the* proofs of moral and social progress and of the superior character of Western civilization and rationality. There could be no better way of expressing this than by maintaining establishments even for those who were devoid of that power of rationality and polite intercourse so highly treasured since the Age of Reason. Insanity itself was in the contemporary mode of expression widely stylized as the 'most grievous malady to which the human family is subject', prompting one medical officer to ask whether there could be 'a more affecting exhibition of suffering than the miserable victim of mental estrangement'.[23] No wonder then, that lunatic asylums, long visited by high-ranking government officials, were soon to become part of travellers' tours of the 'real India', where British stations' first ladies would organize Christmas dinner dances and concerts on the Queen's birthday.

The contemporary view of the European lunatic asylum in India as a showpiece of British humanitarian and scientific progress may strike us as overblown in the light of the small scale of actual provision. But it is to a great extent exactly this overstatement and the disproportionate fervour with which the relevance of the madhouse was advanced that contributed to the maintenance of the self-image of the British as a superior people whose charitable humanitarianism and rational, scientific achievements made colonial rule appear morally beneficial and legitimate. The legitimacy of colonial rule remained as fiercely asserted as it was disputed and, similarly, the institutionalization of the mentally ill remained an important symbolic marker both for enthusiastic advocates and for opponents of an extended British presence in India.

The ideological role of the asylum outlived the Company's administration of East India, persisting up to the heyday of imperial rule, when the confinement of European and Indian lunatics in specialized institutions was implemented on a greater, though still quite modest scale. It appears asylums were still considered an important enough feature of colonial rule to be made an example of: the liberal member of parliament who, to the consternation of the European community, visited British India in order to convince himself of the propriety of continued British rule in the East, was reported to have asked to be taken 'as a preliminary canter, to the goal and lunatic asylum' where 'he will make many interesting suggestions to the civil surgeon as to the management of these institutions, comparing them unfavourably with those he has visited in other stations'.[24] Afterwards, it was held, he 'will probably write his article for the *Twentieth Century*, entitled "Is India worth keeping?"'.

The European madhouse had, of course, not only positive socio-political and symbolic connotations for the expatriate community. Just as the Georgian and Victorian public in Britain was ambivalent towards public institutions and their clientele, so European town dwellers in India were, for example, not particularly eager to accept asylums in close proximity to private residencies. In 1851, citizens of Madras managed to divert the local government's plan to considerably enlarge the then dilapidated buildings. They pleaded that government reconsider the purchase of the property in Kilpauk.[25] An enlarged asylum would not only create a nuisance – even 'great injury' – but also depress local property prices. The area was claimed to be unsuitable as a retreat for the insane: Kilpauk was described as a bustling suburb with the asylum being located close to noisy Indian dwellings, markets and temples. Similarly, when various plans for the new premises of the Bombay asylum were mooted by government in 1853, locations had to be found that would be neither 'near to nuisances such as noisy trades, or offensive manufactures', nor be likely to become 'surrounded or overlook[ed] or be liable to be inconvenienced by the neighbourhood of public roads or foot paths'.[26]

Generally preferred locations for asylums were isolated areas, ideally as separate from the main hub of colonial town life as the island of Salzette in Bombay. However, guaranteeing security for the European and Indian publics and the early nineteenth-century ideal of the asylum as a 'retreat' cannot entirely account for Europeans' tendency to seek isolated locations. The fame of the York Retreat in England (which was situated in pleasing countryside and for a few decades epitomized the last word in asylum construction and enlightened care for the mentally ill) had reached reform-conscious government, medical officials and members of the public in the East. It left its stamp at least on their rhetoric. Lacking geographically secluded spots in the immediate and easily accessible vicinity of towns, it was in suburbs with primarily Indian populations and lower property prices, like Bhowanipur in Calcutta, where asylums were to be found. Lahore's old lunatic asylum, established by Dr John 'Martin Sahib' Honigberger, state physician to Maharaja Dhalip Singh in the early nineteenth century, was situated 'in the heart of the city'.[27] Following the annexation of the Punjab in 1849, the 'unsuitability of the situation' was criticized by the civil surgeon and consequently new premises were provided. It was considered 'a serious inconvenience to have [lunatics] confined in the middle of the civil station' and they were finally moved to a house that was 'outflanked' by the railway station and 'at a considerable distance from any dwelling-house'. As elsewhere, public institutions such as jails, hospitals and lunatic asylums were increasingly – if not separated from the European quarters by the railway – at least placed on the margins of the European parts of town.

Seclusion and isolation implied not merely the separation of the mad from those who considered themselves sane. They came to mean more specifically the separation of the mad from the *European* public. The desire to maintain social distance between those Europeans who thought they were in possession of their wits and those who were considered to have gone 'doolally' was just as strong as the desire to keep people of different social class and racial background apart. Yet the fear of the mentally ill and the wish to keep them well away from European public life were not at all prejudicial to the prevalent tendency to look upon institutions for the mad with pride rather than dismay. The lunatic asylum, inconvenient as its solid presence close to European quarters may have been, was also a relatively secure and impressive means of keeping the mad at bay. Like schools, orphanages, workhouses and the various sorts of hospitals ('general' hospitals for the better-off, police hospitals for down and outs, lock-hospitals for the vice-ridden), asylums for Europeans and Indians had become vital elements by which the *pax Britannica* asserted itself in the East. Surgeon J. Macpherson expressed this when he exclaimed in the 1850s: 'we have our jails, our schools, and our dispensaries in almost every Zillah, and why should we not have our asylums too?'[28]

Towards Uniformity

Macpherson's rhetorical question captures the general feeling amongst most of the European community that the best place to keep the mentally ill was behind the walls of British institutions. By the late 1850s almost every largish *zila* (district) made provision, if not for the European, then at least for the Indian insane on an unprecedented scale. The scale of measures as well as their emergent uniformity and the extent to which institutionalization had become routinized had changed since the beginning of the century. Thus the development of the British Indian madhouse followed the pattern characteristic

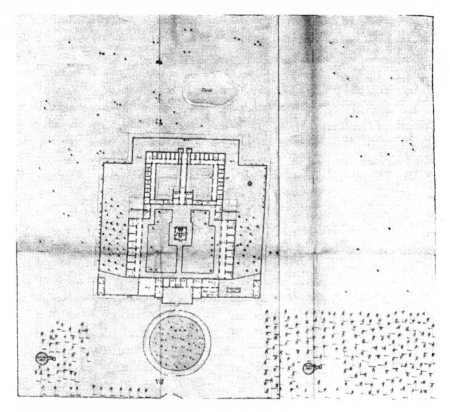

Figure 5. Lunatic Asylum, Madras, 1852 (ground plan).

of the situation in the colonial motherland itself, with organized lunacy provision slowly emerging towards the second half of the nineteenth century from a patchwork of highly diverse and sometimes controversial measures.

The visual representation of the European asylum also underwent a slow homogenization. Within half a century institutions as different externally as the Calcutta Asylum (resembling functional city offices), the Madras Asylum (more basic and gradually shabby-looking in its low-quality army barrack style) and the Bombay Asylum (well-secluded, functional and horseshoe-shaped) would be replaced by or adapted to a modified version of the standard style recommended by the commissioners in lunacy in England. However, madhouses in British India were not mere replicas of institutions in Europe. Nor were they as isomorphous as the mass of buildings constructed by architects and engineers of the reputed public works department. Concessions had to be made to local climatic factors and the quality and comfort of premises varied considerably according to prospective inmates' race and social class.

Although medical and government authorities in India were aware of the necessity to adapt European institutional designs to the 'peculiarities' of the climate and to provide appropriate means of separating various groups among the insane, there was no unanimity as to what a lunatic asylum should look like. Despite the Company's best endeavours, mental institutions in British India were only slowly converging on Victorian uniformity. The author of *Hospitals and Asylums of the World* could therefore maintain as late as 1902 that lunatic asylums in India were of the 'irregular or conglomerate type'.[29] In the first and second half of the nineteenth century the diversity was even greater.

The formal status of institutions underwent a similarly slow and often uncoordinated move towards standardization. Around 1800 the main European lunatic asylums (Madras, Bombay and Calcutta) were all privately owned by medical officers and run as commercial concerns. In Bombay a surgeon, R. Fildes, kept mentally ill European and Indian civilians and military personnel in his private house on the island of Kolaba. They had recently been moved there from a small institution on Butcher's Island. Assistant surgeon Valentine Conolly received the Madras government's insane employees into his private madhouse in Kilpauk. And in Calcutta assistant surgeon W. Dick owned Bengal's then only private lunatic asylum for Europeans. From 1787 he offered his medical services and the lease of his establishment to government.

By the 1830s only the Calcutta asylum was still privately managed. It was supported by the governor-general against the medical board's explicit objections. In Bombay and Madras government and medical officials had, in 1826 and 1808 respectively, virtually abolished the private 'mad-business' and decreed that medical officers were to have no financial interest in the running of the institutions. The authority of the medical board was strengthened in order to thwart corruption and abuse of inmates. By the mid-1850s even the Calcutta asylum had fallen prey to 'nationalization' and from that time onwards all lunatic asylums for Europeans had similar formal status and management structures.

Whether an asylum was privately or publicly owned did not by itself determine conditions inside the institution, nor guarantee cost efficiency. The quality of provision and the state of the buildings appear to have been superior in Calcutta where the asylum was privately run by the Beardsmore family from 1821 to 1856. The Bombay asylum, in contrast, built from public funds in the 1820s and maintained and controlled by government, was described 24 years after its inauguration by its medical superintendent as 'utterly inadequate' and such as to make it 'little short of a miracle that a man ever leaves this hospital cured'.[30] Sanitation had deteriorated, with the drainage and cess-pool system underneath the 'native male wards' resembling 'an augean stable of impurity which it would take the efforts of a Hercules to correct or cleanse'.[31]

Overcrowding posed insuperable difficulties. In 1850, for example, 80 Indian men had to 'be huddled together into a range of apartments originally built and still adapted for the accommodation of not more than 24'.[32] European patients were not affected by overcrowding, as the men (of whom there were but two in 1850) had been allocated one whole ward, which they had to share with only one Eurasian or 'Indo-Briton' and one Portuguese patient.[33] Neither did the 17 female patients suffer from want of space on a ward adapted for the accommodation of 24.[34] Yet their treatment was adversely affected since the asylum's doctor had to spend a considerable proportion of his time in attempts to establish order and discipline on the Indian wards where 'dangerous characters' were 'cooped up' with 'quiet and harmless' inmates.

The situation was even worse in Madras. Here the building had become structurally unsound by the 1840s – only 50 years after it had been constructed as a private enterprise by Conolly. The superintending surgeon described the place in 1846 as being in a 'highly dangerous state,'[35] having originally been built of material of the most inferior quality and 'extremely ill calculated in every way for a Lunatic Asylum'.[36] 'Many of the Cells', he maintained, 'are so inferior in every particular that in England criminals of the worst description would not be confined in them'.[37] Unlike the Beardsmores' asylum in Calcutta, parts of which survived well into the twentieth century, Conolly's madhouse had by the middle of the nineteenth century become 'incapable of restoration'.[38] This was a blow to the Madras authorities, as they had within half a century invested the large sum of three and a half *lakh* of Rupees (Rs 350,000) for the building in rent alone. By comparison, the estimated construction cost of the new Madras lunatic asylum, completed in 1871, amounted to a mere one and a half *lakh* or 150,000 Rupees. What is more, the local government had originally provided the land on which Conolly's institution was built and paid the salary of the European staff. From 1823 onwards the institution had been 'private' only formally, as the former owner's heirs to whom he had bequeathed the building engaged an agent to administer the routine affairs of the property and negotiate with government.[39] Nevertheless, no major improvements in the building were undertaken. The supreme government in Bengal declined the local Madras authorities' wish to erect badly needed new premises and the once flourishing enterprise went into gradual decay so that towards the middle of the century European patients of the higher classes would usually no longer be admitted.

Asylum reformers in England and India strongly favoured the passing of private institutions into public hands on grounds of the anticipated improved surveillance of patients' condition and the prevention of suspected abuse. Of the three asylums for Europeans, it was however the privately owned and managed

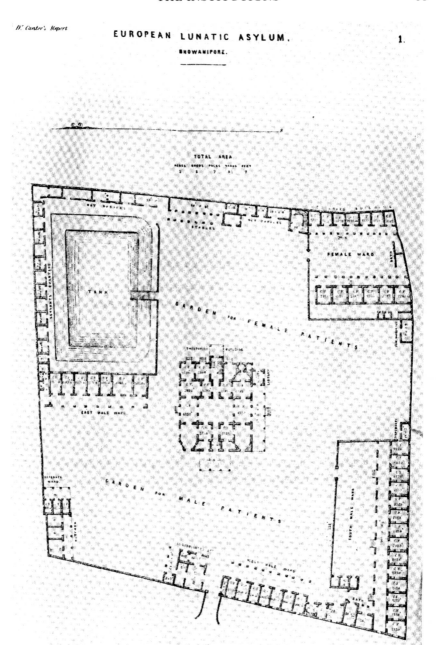

Figure 6. European Lunatic Asylum, Calcutta, early nineteenth century.

Calcutta asylum that was to make provision on a comparatively adequate and constant level. In 1856, it too was taken over by government. From then onwards it enjoyed the mixed blessing so often typical of public sector establishments and shared by the asylums in Madras and Bombay: increased surveillance of accounts and management practices, on the one hand, and deterioration of the quality of provision for patients of the lower classes, on the other.

Patients' life inside the three main asylums during the early years depended largely on the medical officers' personal styles of management, motivation for the job and their professional expertise and approach to treatment. The Indian medical service offered ample scope for individuals' initiative, especially prior to its reorganization by autocratic Lord Dalhousie. This can be poignantly illustrated by reference to one of the Bombay medicos' devotion to his work. William Campbell, assistant surgeon and asylum superintendent at Kolaba, was instrumental in pressing upon government the necessity of enlarged asylum premises and also took great interest in his patients' illness and even in their former personal lives and problems. The case-reports that he sent to Pembroke House in London were outstanding. They were most elaborate and testified to Campbell's empathy with his patients' woes. Such personal and professional virtues, in Campbell's case verified by his patients' gratitude, was not ubiquitous. As evidenced by flimsy case-descriptions and lack of data on individual inmates, the medical officers in charge of the asylum in Madras were less involved in the care of their protégés than Campbell.

In Calcutta, in contrast, the Beardsmores' humanity and sense of duty had been reported by the medical board to have received favourable comment by the more distinguished among their patients; but indignation was also expressed at the Beardsmores' lack of an 'intimate' and 'cultivated' knowledge of asylum science.[40] Only a few years previously, however, patients had suffered considerably inferior conditions and uncaring treatment. One of the Beardsmores' predecessors, surgeon J. Sawers, had made provision for the province's lunatics in a place that was described as 'damp, sultry and gloomy'.[41] According to Mr I. Beardsmore's evidence, Sawers tended not to turn up when called for emergencies and failed to carry out routine visitations.

Such diversity in asylum conditions and patient-doctor relations in early nineteenth-century India was facilitated by the relative lack of centralized administrative direction and professional regulation. Diversity and experiment were not always considered to be a bad thing. Eminent government officials such as Elphinstone and Munro argued the case against a structure of government that they feared would become 'a state of dull uniform repose'[42] and stressed that 'our government should still be considered as in a great measure experimental; and it is an advantage to have three experiments [in Bengal, Madras and Bombay], and to compare them in their progress with each other'.[43] Each of the specific approaches to the treatment of the insane could also be more or less convincingly justified by reference to one or other of the numerous methods that mushroomed in England. The early part of the nineteenth century was the time of diverse experiments in the management and the medical and psychological treatment of the insane. No standard technique had as yet emerged, nor was any single theory of the causation and cure of mental illness accepted by the Anglo-Saxon scientific community. What one doctor proudly claimed to have used with success was disparaged by the next.

This situation was to change drastically by the middle of the century. The tendency towards uniformity of asylum management and provision is captured by the general attention to detail, evidenced in the asylum rules devised for European lunatic asylums in India in 1856 by surgeon T. Cantor of Calcutta.[44] Cantor was firmly convinced of the need to clearly establish a hierarchical chain of command amongst the staff. He accordingly drew up separate sets of rules for the guidance of the asylum's subordinate officers (usually consisting of a matron, apothecary, steward and two overseers) and the 'native establishment' (consisting in the case of the 80 patient Calcutta asylum of about 70 to 80 employees of different status, representing trades as diverse as that of keepers, watchmen, servants, cleaners and ladies' maids as well as cooks, gardeners, water-carriers, carpenters and tailors). The hierarchical order was headed by Cantor himself, to whom subordinate officers had to report the general state on the wards and, on occasion of his twice-daily visitation, any emergencies and irregularities. The Indian staff was to communicate with him only through the mediation of the head keeper, who in turn would first call on one of the subordinate officers.

Surgeon Cantor further intended to have the lunatic asylum hermetically sealed from the preying eye of the public. Patients were forbidden to cultivate any contact with people outside the asylum and subordinates were responsible for submitting any 'communications to or from the patients' to the superintendent.[45] Similarly, servants were explicitly required 'not secretly to carry letters, messages or articles to or from the Patients'. For the first time in the history of the European lunatic asylum in India the flow of information between asylum inmates and the outside world was considerably curtailed. Above all, nobody apart from the superintendent was entitled to respond to 'enquiries concerning the Patients or the Institution'.

The intention was to turn the asylums into what Goffman termed 'total institutions'. The Indian staff was even forbidden to 'talk loudly' and was required to undergo the patronizing ordeal of having to listen to a 'Bengallee translation' of the asylum rules during the monthly muster.[46] The keepers' day and night watch routines were meticulously laid down. Nine of them had to be on duty in the wards from 8 a.m. to 4 p.m. and from 4 p.m. to 8 a.m. respectively.

Theirs was mainly a controlling and disciplining duty. During the night they had to 'go round all the wards every quarter of an hour, to ascertain that the Patients are in their rooms'. During the day they had to 'prevent the Patients from leaving the wards between the hours of out door exercise'. The specific duties of the subordinate officers were less rigidly circumscribed; it was seen to be 'impracticable concisely to define the duties of each individual'. Instead they were 'readily and cheerfully to render their assistance, whenever required'.

Even the hitherto customary practice of having the superintendent reside within the confines of the asylum premises and thus within easy reach and open sight of patients, was strongly questioned by Cantor on grounds that

> while living absolutely in the midst of the patients, and being thus brought almost hourly into contact with them, his authority and general efficiency become abridged and impaired, his intercourse with them being virtually rather that of a keeper than of a Supervisor.[47]

For the sake of the increased discipline expected to be occasioned by physical distance between superintendent and patients, Cantor was permitted to reside in separate apartments. He vacated his previous quarters for the use of subordinate officers whose authority and respect were apparently not expected to suffer by close contact with inmates.

Admittedly, reforms other than those directed at reduced transparency of the institution and tightened discipline among staff and patients had also been effected by Cantor. He emphasized that 'unwearied kindness is under all circumstances to prevail in the treatment of the Patients' and that the 'native Servants, male and female' have to 'abstain from harsh language, threats, abuse, blows and all other acts of oppression or violence'.[48] Professional inspection, too, was guaranteed to a certain extent, as members of the medical board and the chief magistrate were admitted to examine asylum records. However, asylum visitations had, in principle, been part of government officials' duty prior to Cantor and the requirement to treat asylum inmates with humanity and kindness had been expressed by many superintendents before him. Even Mr I. Beardsmore, who had frequently been criticized by the medical board as an 'industrious but uneducated man', had been familiar with the jargon of the period and had emphasized the necessity of 'moral management', 'non-restraint' and 'humane and kind' treatment.[49] Nor was the talk of discipline and order altogether unheard of before Cantor's time. What, however, made a difference was the extent to which particular regimes were being implemented by Cantor. For example, within only four months he brought the expenditure on account of second-class patients down to half by economizing on their diet – an innovation that was according to Cantor met by 'no complaint'.[50]

The change effected by Cantor in the 1850s was on balance one for the worse from the point of view of second-class inmates. The differences become particularly obvious if his asylum rules are contrasted with those that had officially been in force in the three European asylums around 1800. The regulations for the Bengal lunatic hospital that had been drawn up in 1789 for Dick's asylum in Calcutta, for example, consisted mainly of a guideline for proper classification of patients.[51] Patients were divided into five different classes. For each class the superintendent was allowed to charge a particular rate, which was usually commensurable with the patients' former social background. Subaltern officers were worth their former pay and *batta* (special allowances). For sergeants and privates, too, the superintendent was allowed to draw the amount of their pay and *batta*. Persons who had not been affiliated to the Company's service were seen to 'have no particular claim upon Government'. Those in the 'character of Gentlemen' were therefore downgraded from the initially suggested Rs 176 – the equivalent of a Lieutenant's pay and *batta* – to Rs 100. Poor Europeans were in contrast classified like privates. And, finally, for ladies the money drawn by the superintendent from the Company's accounts amounted to the equivalent of a Lieutenant's pay, namely around Rs 176.

The rules about financial arrangements were supplemented with further guidelines concerning asylum management in general. The Bombay authorities for example specified that the provision with 'Stocks, Hand-cuffs +ca' was to be guaranteed by the Company and, like those of Madras, they stipulated: 'The Hospital...be at all times open to the Inspection of the members of the Medical Board, and to the Civil Magistrate, but to no other Person, without a Ticket from the Surgeon'.[52] Yet, there was no provision made that would *ensure* the regular inspection of the premises. Similarly, the Bengal medical board had in 1821 drawn up more detailed regulations that referred to such essential details as admission and discharge procedures, visitations, medication, patients' clothing, bedding, diet, recreation and record keeping. The superintendent of the day, Mr I. Beardsmore, however never assented to these. In his outright rejection of official control he was supported by government and was consequently allowed to pursue his own regime.

With Cantor's appointment as superintendent of the supreme province's only European lunatic asylum the stern spirit of discipline, internal control, regimentation and financial economy came to pervade this institution's hitherto more open and permissive atmosphere. By the 1860s Cantor's innovations had diffused throughout British India and become part and parcel of nearly all asylum regimes. Daily food rations were then officially prescribed and dished out to the ounce and patients' segregation and classification were strictly and uniformly enforced. The lunatic asylum had become a place where, as Foucault put it, 'order no longer freely confronted disorder, reason no longer tried to make its own way among all that might evade or seek to destroy it'.[53]

Inside the Institutions

Asylum conditions deteriorated towards the middle of the century, though the higher-class European insane were only slightly affected. They had never really been deprived of the facilities and comfort their social position was assumed to demand. They had always been lodged in superior apartments, separate from the madding crowd on the wards. Their diet, clothing and means of recreation were generous. They were waited upon by personal servants and – when nearing convalescence – enjoyed some freedom of movement and occasional polite company of the superintendent. In the Beardsmores' asylum in Calcutta, for example, they frequently dined at the family table. In Bombay surgeon Campbell regularly went for walks at the beach with them, engaging in small-talk and enjoying the superb panorama of the city's harbour with its sailing-ships against the backdrop of the hills that could be glimpsed on the horizon. A patients' library (in Calcutta even equipped with a *punkah* or fan), was made available for first-class inmates. Reading material such as the *Illustrated News*, *The Times*, and *Punch* was on offer, along with amusements like chess, draughts, backgammon, domino, kaleidoscopes and, occasionally, music.[54]

The Madras higher-class patients were more seriously affected by the decline in institutional conditions. By the middle of the century the building there had come so close to dereliction that alternative accommodation had to be found. Even then every effort was made to provide conditions for first-class patients conducive to their physical comfort and peace of mind. Captain John C. of Madras, for example, acquitted of a charge of murder on account of his state of mind, was allocated a whole wing in the jail, the asylum being by then considered 'unsuited for persons of his class'.[55] In order to maintain his comfort and the safety of those around him, the other inmates were made to squeeze up in the remaining smaller part of the institution and the staff suffered even greater than normal difficulties in maintaining order.

The deterioration of the buildings of the Bombay asylum was not as bad as in Madras. But overcrowding here too was a problem and conditions were bad enough for the medical board to express their indignation. 'Treatment, whether moral, medical, or hygienic' was considered to be 'surrounded by difficulties, all but unsuperable'.[56] Various projects to ameliorate this situation, such as the transfer of intellectually disabled patients to a specially designed 'village of imbeciles', were considered. In 1850 'harmless idiots', the 'fatuous' and 'imbeciles' (as the intellectually disabled were called) made up about 55 per cent of the asylum population. Had they been boarded out, the asylum's overcrowding would have been considerably alleviated.[57] Another option considered was to confine 'criminal lunatics' in separate premises. This, too, would have greatly eased the pressure on the European lunatic asylum, as the criminal lunatics acts of 1849 and 1851 had driven up their numbers. Another alternative canvassed was to allocate a separate institution to 'insane native soldiers' and to fill up any arising vacancies with 'criminal lunatics'; or to keep the existing institution as a depot for Europeans *en route* to repatriation and construct a new asylum for the remaining Indian and Eurasian patients.

Any of these suggestions would have alleviated the conditions in the Bombay asylum, but they would have been costly. A more straightforward cost-saving measure would have been to simply change the system of classification and segregation that by itself exacerbated overcrowding. Two of the four wards designed to accommodate between 12 and 17 inmates, were allocated to 'native males', one to females and another to Europeans.[58] In 1850, 17 female patients were confined without problem on a ward of their own. The second ward, too, could hardly have been considered congested with only four patients of 'European habits'. The remaining 80 patients (80 per cent of the asylum population, exclusively Indians and lower-class Eurasians) were left with only half the building.

The superintendent pointed out that the bare statistics did not convey 'an adequate conception of the real nature and magnitude of the disproportion which actually exists'.[59] He went on to explain that

of these 80 lunatics there are eight whose symptoms and peculiarities are such as to render it absolutely indispensable that they should each be confined in a separate place so that 16 cells only are left for the accommodation of 72 individuals.

Since each of those cells measured only two by three metres, the superintendent's concern that Victorian precepts of decency and morality as well as the effectiveness of treatment and the security of inmates were at stake, appear well founded. 'The case is still further aggravated', he wrote in his petition for new asylum premises to government,

when we consider the total disregard for decency and propriety which those afflicted with insanity so frequently manifest. Their propensities are often filthy and disgusting in the extreme – they go about naked – they obey the calls of nature wherever they are sitting or laying, and I leave it to the imagination of the reader to depict what must be the state of premises so limited, crowded with human beings, many of whom have habits so revolting – surely this requires no comment.

Such inadequacies made the 'treatment and cure of the most grievous malady to which the human family is subject' difficult. '[C]ould it', the surgeon asked, 'be wondered at, had I 'ere another day has run its course, to report a murder or a suicide within these walls?'[60]

Although conditions in the Bombay asylum appear to have been bad, it was mainly the Indian and Eurasian insane who bore the brunt of them as officials insisted on race-, class- and gender-specific segregation. Even as the medical officer in charge of the institution pressed government to lose no time 'in doing something to ameliorate the condition of the unhappy wretches' on his wards, he himself would not even contemplate a change in classificatory practice.[61] Even though he had explained that 'inmates could theoretically be accommodated without problems, if they were equally distributed over the different parts of the premises', he noted that 'difference of sex, caste, and color, rendered this of course...altogether impossible'.[62] European first-class patients certainly suffered some of the inconvenience that necessarily went along with the fact of their apartments' close proximity to wards that were characterized by a critic in the local newspaper as being in an 'abominable' state, resembling 'dungeons'. Apart from this, however, they experienced little deprivation.

For European second-class patients things were more variable, depending mainly on who was in charge. Surgeon Campbell, for example, usually showed them respect, kindness and consideration, albeit adapted to their 'former habits and tastes'.[63] Gunner Francis H., one of Campbell's patients who had been admitted to the Bombay asylum in 1852 as a 'maniac', believing he was the 'spirit of the immortal Byron', expressed his feeling of 'gratitude for the kindly interest' shown to him by the superintendent. Being fully aware of the social gulf between himself and the medical officer, H. pointed out that this interest 'becomes more affecting from the infrequency of the exhibition of such a feeling from a superior towards an inferior'.[64] Some of Campbell's predecessors were indeed less inclined to show any 'kindly interest' to patients of the 'lower orders of society'.

In no other asylum than in Calcutta had the quality of provision and life within the institution been more varied, being explicitly dependent on inmates' social standing and racial background. The metropolis of the supreme province of Bengal – the acclaimed 'city of palaces' – had by the early nineteenth century taken over the role of trend-setter from Madras. In particular in terms of social precedence and class-consciousness, the European community in Calcutta was first to develop and last to give up hardened attitudes bordering on snobbery and bigotry. The climate of racial and social intolerance inevitably permeated the lunatic asylum. The European asylum in Calcutta had an advantage over the institutions in Madras and Bombay in that its superintendents needed to take no pains to create social distance and racial segregation. The Calcutta asylum from

1821 onwards admitted only European and higher-class Eurasian patients (except in exceptional circumstances, as in the case of mentally ill members of the Indian royalty). 'Assembling Europeans and Natives in one Establishment' was in the words of the medical board, in 1847, a 'crude and incongruous scheme'.[65] A couple of decades earlier, in 1821, the board had strongly objected to the Company's court's suggestion that authorities in India 'dispose of the few cases of Insanity in Europeans' by temporarily keeping them in the 'native lunatic asylum' near Calcutta.[66] The 'propriety of mixing Europeans labouring under mental derangement with natives in the same unfortunate condition' was, the medical board held, 'very questionable'.[67] Racial segregation was consequently sustained inter-institutionally and separate lunatic asylums for Indians and lower-class Eurasians were to be found from the beginning of the nineteenth century in the major districts: Benares, Bareilly, Patna, Dacca and near Calcutta, and, towards the middle of the century, in Delhi.

Although the superintendents in the Calcutta asylum at Bhowanipore escaped the task of separating Indians and Europeans, they were still careful to make appropriate provision for Europeans and Eurasians of different gender and social backgrounds. By the late 1850s the asylum consisted of 'two divisions': one for male, the other for female patients.[68] In all, 63 single rooms were available on the various wards. As the number of patients was by that time on average about 80, second-class patients had to share a cell. Each of these was provided with a window 'well out of reach' and with 'an iron barred door' – the latter allowed the 'free circulation of Air' and was seen as 'preferable to the solid doors with inspection plates' then common in England. The ventilation device without which no reasonably well-to-do European household in India would make do, the man-powered *punkah*, was however absent in patients' rooms. Cells were not 'lofty' enough to allow their installation, explained Surgeon Cantor in 1856. It seems, however, that the cost involved in the maintenance of an establishment of *punkah-wallahs* was not an altogether irrelevant factor, especially when patients were more easily 'supplied with a palm leaf fan', which they could operate themselves and the expense of which was negligible, being only 'one pice a piece'.

The rooms for second-class patients were spartanly furnished. Wooden bed-steads, similar to those used in European barracks and hospitals were provided. The floors were un-matted, so that they could be conveniently cleaned and allow for 'baths being applied whenever required'. The only other chattels were 'bed utensils' in case of an inmate's physical disease or manic fits.[69] Violent or ill second-class patients had to stay in their cells at all times, while for the other inmates the rooms opened on to the adjoining verandah, which was 'screened by venetians and canvas curtains'. Tables were spread there for the meals and lamps were lighted at night. The more tractable patients would spend most of the time during the 'heat of the day and in wet weather' on these 'common Verandahs'. Each ward was equipped with one 'easily accessible and ample privy and bathing room with shower Baths'. Only in the case of first-class patients, in their superior, separate apartments, was the fact that they had to share the toilet and bathing facilities with ward patients an issue.

Although nowhere near to the abysmal conditions in Madras and Bombay, 'want of space and accommodation' was by the 1850s in Calcutta also seen as the main obstacle to patients' classification in accordance with their state of mind.[70] The lack of 'isolated wards for refractory patients' in particular was lamented by the medical officer in charge. 'A single violent patient', he argued, 'is sure to produce a number of imitations and to keep the asylum in an uproar, as long as the paroxysm may last'. The benefit all patients were considered to gain from exercise and walks in the garden was in practice available only to a small number of them and then only for a short time twice a day. The garden, though 'remarkably well laid out', was 'too limited' in extent, 'particularly considering the number of Patients and the paramount importance of extensive pleasure grounds in all Lunatic Asylums'.

Constricted space and overcrowding were perceived as detrimental to both treatment and order. Notorious understaffing was also criticized. Keepers and servants were not 'less essential than cells' for the control and safety of asylum inmates – and there were occasions when safety was endangered by a lack of staff.[71] The intensity of care shown by the staff, too, was not always satisfactory. Complaints centred not only on the 'native servants', in none of whom surgeon Cantor, for example, would 'place confidence'.[72] Subordinate personnel, usually invalid European soldiers or young Eurasians, were frequently criticized for neglect or incompetence. It had been common practice until the middle of the century for staff to be hired 'by the day or week like common labourers' and this, as pointed out by the medical board in 1836, had adverse consequences for patients. A 'sufficiency of Male and Female keepers...permanently engaged and taught by experience and appropriate instruction to manage persons suffering under various forms of mental derangement' was 'indispensable to an Institution worthy of the patronage of Government'.[73]

The peculiarities of the Indian climate and the characteristics of British expatriates exposed to an alien culture in a colonial situation necessitated modifications in asylum regimes. Arguments from cultural preference and racial propensity were advanced by medical officers in India to explain the absence of one highly lauded aspect of the 'moral management' of the insane then popular in Britain: patients' engagement in productive work. 'Remedial employment' was considered to be 'utterly inapplicable in tropical India, where the climate renders farming, gardening and occupation in the Kitchen, laundry or bakehouse impracticable, if not injurious to Europeans'.[74] The detrimental effect of manual labour was one of few peculiarly colonial factors that cut across the lines of social class. 'To the Majority of the Patients at Bhowanipore, Soldiers, Sailors and Gentlemen' alike, mechanical labour was expected to be 'uncongenial'. In India the employment of European inmates was consequently considered to produce exactly the opposite effect to that in Britain.

Non-Europeans, in contrast, were believed to benefit from active work, although in their case, too, racial and cultural differences were taken into account. Surgeon Cantor had, for example, after 'some five months perseverance' succeeded in 'introducing a system of moral treatment, not by compulsion, but by persuasion and well timed rewards' into the Dullunda native lunatic asylum, near Calcutta.[75] His patients, 'some 300 of the poorer classes of Bengallees', were made to pluck hemp or coir, make ropes, swabs and rugs, spin wool for blankets or work in the kitchens and gardens. In contrast to asylum inmates in South East Asia, where Cantor had previously been on duty, Indian patients were apparently less amenable to such 'moral treatment'. Cantor found the introduction of 'voluntary manual labour' to have been 'a task less easy to accomplish at Dullunda than it proved in the Lunatic Asylum at Pinang in 1843', where the patients had been 'Malays, Chinese, Klings, Burmese, Siamese, Cochin-Chinese and Hindostanees'. According to Cantor they 'took Kindlier to a variety of light work than has been found the case with the Bengallees'. Similarly, Eurasian patients were thought to loathe manual work. According to a common British stereotype they were 'scribblers', or *crannies*, dedicated to secretarial work, and who therefore 'despised all trades, save that of the desk'. Eurasian inmates in the Calcutta asylum, who were seen to 'evince their habitual propensity to scribbling', were therefore supplied with slates in order 'to save paper and walls'.

A regulated time-table and daily routine were considered no less important than activity for moral treatment and could easily be implemented. In Calcutta where life inside the asylum had been strictly organized by Cantor from the late 1950s onwards, an uninspiring daily routine prevailed:

The patients rise at gunfire, and are taken for an hour's walk round the garden. Bath and Toilet over, the superintendent pays his Morning visit. The Breakfast and Dinner hours are at 8 and 2 o'Clock. About half an hour before sunset, after the evening visit, the Patients take exercise in the garden. Tea is served at 7. At 8 or not later than 9 o'Clock, the Patients are in bed. The hours intervening between the meals, are filled up according to the condition and fancy of each Patient, in reading, games, conversation, or sleep. Quiet patients are admitted in the Steward's Office, which is also made to serve as reading room and library.[76]

In the long intervals during which inmates were left to themselves, time must have hung heavily on their hands. This was not altogether uncommon in Europeans' life in India outside the asylum. Military servants, for example, found that being confined to their barracks most of the day tended to 'get on their nerves', in particular during the hot season when temperatures soared and they had to 'sweat it out'. The soldiers would lie on their *charpoys* or beds in the barrack-rooms, 'many of them naked, under a mosquito net to keep the flies off, and the only thing moving was the *punkah* above them going backwards and forwards, backwards and forwards'.[77] Widespread as such ennui was known to be, steps towards an amelioration of the situation were taken, neither for the rank and file in the military, nor for lower-class lunatics in the asylums.

The question then arises as to what effect, if any, confinement in one of the three European madhouses had on its inmates' condition?[78] No answer as to the effects of the workings of the asylum regime on patients' minds and wellbeing is easily gleaned from the few case-reports produced within the institutions. Nor do the scanty accounts by outsiders such as the reputed asylum reformer Sir Andrew Halliday, or by the lesser known Dr G. A. Berwick, provide more reliable information. One may therefore be tempted to conclude that circumstances were similar to those alluded to by the early eighteenth-century traveller (and interloper) Captain Alexander Hamilton in respect to the hospital in Calcutta. Hamilton mused sardonically: 'The Company has a pretty good Hospital at Calcutta, where many go in to undergo the Penance of Physick but few come out to give account of its Operation'.[79]

One alternative way of approaching the question would be to analyze the statistics that medical boards and asylum superintendents devised on cure, discharge and mortality rates. From the asylums' inception superintendents had been obliged to draw up statistics. During the early decades of the nineteenth century these consisted mainly of rolls, providing only basic data such as inmates' name, age, profession, date of admission and discharge. Towards the middle of the century medical officers gradually started to put numerical values on their proteges' condition. This process was unreliable and subject to miscalculation. Conceptual problems abounded. The decision when to declare a patient as 'cured', 'relieved', or 'uncured' was based more on guess-work and wishful thinking than on accurate diagnostics. With these caveats, which apply to all early nineteenth-century institutional numerical records, the statistics provided for asylums in British India frequently compared well with those supplied by public institutions in Britain. For example, the total percentage of people discharged as 'cured' from the European asylum in Bengal from 1824 to 1850 lies at 36 per cent, only slightly below the rates then common in madhouses in England and Wales.[80]

More problematic were statistics on the number of 'long-term' patients and 'incurable' cases. In the late 1840s it was revealed that a comparatively large number of inmates in the Calcutta asylum had been there for long periods, some for over 20 years. In December 1847, for example, when the statistics showed a total of 43 inmates, 16 lunatics had been confined for more than seven years.[81] In England, a similar tendency towards long-term institutionalization had emerged in the late 1840s and 1850s. The gradual crowding of institutions with 'chronic cases' contributed to more pessimism as to the possibility of curing insanity and caused the authorities to demand more detailed statistics in order to establish asylums' cure- and cost-effectiveness. The medical authorities in Bengal found it difficult to meet this demand, posing, as it did, the problems of defining constructs such as 'incurability', which notionally implied a well-grounded knowledge of the nature of insanity and of susceptibility of diverse forms of mental illness to medical treatment and institutional intervention. Such considerations had not to date preoccupied the medical professionals' let alone the asylum proprietors' minds to any great extent. The problem was consequently evaded by stating 'as the nearest approximation to a calculation that those who have been above two years in the Asylum may safely be pronounced incurable'.[82]

The data gained on this basis were again very similar to those for England. In both cases the questionable criterion of 'time spent inside an institution' as an indicator of 'incurability' reflects the contemporary belief in the institution as the appropriate measure for the cure of the temporarily insane and reliance on the long-term confinement of 'hopeless' cases. Time spent within the very institution that was designed for the cure and confinement of mental illness had become an allegedly objective criterion for the probability of hopelessness!

Circumstances in British India differed in one important aspect from those in Britain. The majority of European patients were routinely transferred back to Europe. The bulk of 'long-term patients' was therefore, in the case of the Calcutta asylum, for example, made up of Eurasians 'of the lower and middle classes', namely 'petty tradesmen and paupers', and in that of the Madras and Bombay asylums, of Eurasians and Indians.[83] This racial specificity tended to drastically affect cure and mortality rates. Patients whose relatives were described by the Bombay asylum superintendent as 'poor, ignorant, and superstitious'[84] reached the asylum only when 'the time has, in most instances, long passed during which advantage of any kind could be expected from appropriate scientific treatment'.[85] Similarly, European military lunatics would frequently be detained for up to a year in regimental hospitals before they were sent to the Calcutta asylum. Factors such as these induced the medical board of Bengal to maintain that there existed 'no opportunity in the majority of instances, for ascertaining the effect of treatment in the Asylum'.

Nevertheless, data were provided and despite being deemed hardly comparable, they were set against statistics on institutions in England. Perhaps this was done because in most cases the Indian statistics did not fare badly. The rate of cure (the percentage of cured cases to admissions) had in the Calcutta asylum, for example, averaged about 21 per cent during the period from 1824 to 1850.[86] From 1824 to 1834 it had risen as high as 30 per cent; during the following ten years it decreased to about 16 per cent, reaching a low of 12 per cent towards the late 1840s. Some asylum reformers in England believed that, with adequate institutional care, as many as 60 per cent of the mentally ill could be cured. To do justice to the Calcutta asylum, it should be set against metropolitan, county or military and naval asylums in England and Wales rather than prestigious and selective special institutions such as the York Retreat or Bethlem Royal Hospital. Even the Calcutta asylum's lowest cure-rate of 12 per cent (for the 1840s) bears comparison with a rate of only 11 per cent in English and Welsh military and naval asylums. The average rate for metropolitan and county asylums was 15 and 20 per cent, respectively.[87] Whilst better than the rates in Calcutta, they were of the same order. In 1860 the variation of cure rates among various types of asylums in England and Wales was considerably less, with an average rate of 13 per cent and a steady 11 per cent for naval and military asylums. By that date asylums in Britain, as in British India, had been affected drastically by the accumulation of 'chronic' cases.

Only in regard to mortality rates did asylums in India compare unfavourably with institutions in the British Isles. The mortality rate in the Bengal asylum, for example, increased steadily and during the earlier decades of the nineteenth century it had been on average twice as high for second-class patients.[88] By 1850 it had reached an alarming 18 per cent, with less divergence in the rates for first- and second-class patients (15 and 19 per cent respectively). Such figures were well above the norm for England where 'all large and well conducted asylums together' (such as the York Retreat, Bethlem, St Luke's and Hanwell) were reported to have had an annual mortality-rate of only nine to 10 per cent.[89] Whilst these may sound high by today's standards and compared to the aspirations of early nineteenth-century English asylum reformers, in the contemporary English and the Indian context they were not so alarming. Mortality rates in England during the first half of the century showed a wide variation and in India public institutions in general were notorious for high death-rates.[90] In the 'Tirhoot Jail', for example, mortality in 1851 had been as high as 18 to 20 per cent. In Delhi Jail the figure was considerably lower, namely around 11 per cent. This was still way above an estimated average rate of about three per cent for the town population.[91]

As compared to conditions in other institutions in India as well as in a variety of less specialized English asylums, the madhouses in India do not appear to have been out of the ordinary. Professional aspirations in British India continued to grow and particularly towards the middle of the century some medical officers' aim was to 'bring the insane out of themselves and into contact with all in nature or art or social arrangements that is pleasurable and pure and good'.[92] Needless to say, such ambitions were in the case of lower-class and 'native' lunatics hardly likely to be realized by confinement under the conditions and regimes prevailing in Indian institutions.

Notwithstanding a tendency towards uniformity under state regulation, institutional provision for the care and control of the European insane in India was proximately determined by the idiosyncrasies of madhouse keepers and medical superintendents. These in turn were conditioned by the gender, racial and class mores of the British colonialists, as well as by adaptations of the views on the insane and their treatment prevalent in the British motherland. Institutional discipline, segregative control of inmates, financial considerations and the maintenance of the rulers' image characterized the Company's *pagal-khana* or madhouse. A large number of mentally ill Europeans were apparently dealt with in jails, hospitals and in the community, with fewer passing through the portals of a specialized institution. Nevertheless, lunatic asylums played a significant role in the socio-political infrastructure of the Raj and in its ideological legitimation.

Chapter 4

THE MEDICAL PROFESSION

The Search for Fortune and Professional Recognition

In many pre-modern societies the signification of madness encompassed a wide range of conflicting feelings and psychological projections. The mad could be revered or feared as bearers of preternatural powers, they could be despised as monstrous brutes. The apparent 'simpletons' among them could be romantically idealized as holy, innocent fools or 'naturals', or be ridiculed as village idiots and subjected to atrocities and mean tricks. Those suffering from a more violent strain of madness or melancholic gloominess tended to be approached with the cautious curiosity that is frequently fuelled by admiration and fear – a mixture that might easily find a cathartic release in abuse and brutality, or be converted into veneration. These diverse responses to madness could prevail simultaneously, or one particular attitude might dominate.

Those treating or caring for the mad tended to share the stigma attached to their charges. Just like the mad they were subject to quickly changing perceptions oscillating between respect and suspicion. In the late eighteenth century, this cautious and even hostile attitude can partially be accounted for by the fact that madhouse superintendents rarely possessed any formal medical qualification. They not uncommonly included clergymen and 'quacks', as well as the medically qualified. Until the passing of the Lunatics Act of 1845 obliged each county in England to build its own public lunatic asylum, most madhouses were private investments. This did not help to reduce mad-doctors' ambivalent social image and generally low professional repute. It was widely held by both the public and medical professionals such as A. Duncan (professor of medical jurisprudence at Edinburgh) that '[f]ew speculations can be more unpleasant than that of a private mad-house, and it is seldom if ever undertaken, unless with the hope of receiving large returns on the capital advanced'.[1]

The charge was made by social critics such as Sir Andrew Halliday that madhouse owners were 'wholesale dealers and traffickers' in a particular 'species of human misery'.[2] John Conolly suspected that 'the prospect of certain profit' attracted the ignorant and uneducated and those who were 'capable of no feeling but a desire for wealth'.[3] As a result, mad-doctors with a medical background were keen to accentuate the rational and scientific medical expertise they believed their profession to have acquired with the Enlightenment. By the 1840s the medical profession as a whole had achieved the aim of being – at least in the eyes of the law – acknowledged as the highest faculty and the sole experts in matters of healing. They had established their own professional associations and laid down regulations for medical training. By the late 1850s they had taken steps against the trading of medical qualifications and begun to publish scientific journals and conference proceedings.

Yet, despite the formal trappings of professionalization and progressive medicalization, those doctors involved in the superintendence of madhouses did not for many decades enjoy the high status accorded to what in the vernacular came to be known as the 'demi-gods in white'. Within the discipline of medicine as a whole, psychiatry occupied a marginal position and those medical doctors who were involved in the care of the mad were met with barely concealed suspicion and condescension by their own colleagues. During the second half of the nineteenth century experts in lunacy still had to concede that they specialized 'in a department of science the first principles of which are not recognized by their medical brethren'.[4]

In Britain the rise of the medical profession (and in particular of the mad-doctor) to professional autonomy and expert status had been a slow process, marred by charges of financial embezzlement, inefficiency and abuse of patients, and protracted by setbacks in legal battles against members of the less well-connected healing arts, such as bone-setters, and 'quacks'. The social and professional status of the medical officers of the East India Company was even more ambivalent and the nature of their expertise was the subject of a great deal of controversy. Graphic accounts were given of medicos' backgrounds and abilities, which did not fail to capture people's imagination. The claim that a 'butcher got a Surgeon's certificate' in 1758 is but one pertinent example.[5] Chevers' anecdote, related in 1854, of the '*Philosophic* Surgeon who on his way to his indigo factory would enquire of the native doctor – "Any thing to-day" – and, upon receiving the ready answer, "All's well, Lord of the world, only five men dead", would exclaim cheerfully – "good, very good" – and canter gaily about his business', is another.[6]

A good many such stories were certainly exaggerated, but they contained a grain of truth. Up to the late eighteenth century, candidates for the medical services were nominated by the directors of the East India Company and, until 1800, the London Corporation of Surgeons issued what was considered to be an inferior diploma qualifying applicants for appointments as hospital mate or assistant surgeon in an Indian province. Although in 1773 a professorial board had been established in London to examine candidates for the Company's medical service, this did not prevent aspirants from having recourse to less arduous ways of obtaining an appointment in the Orient, as evidenced by an advert in *The Times* of 6 March 1806:

FIFTY POUNDS may be had by procuring the Advertiser an ASSISTANT SURGEONCY in the East India Company's service. Address (postpaid) to A.M., at Peele's Coffee-House.[7]

What prospective appointees such as 'the Advertiser' were after was frequently not so much professional satisfaction as a medical officer, but the potentially large fortunes to be made in the East. The residency surgeoncy at Lucknow in 1785, for example, was estimated to have brought in as much as Rs 8,000 per month – a tidy sum, largely made up of the allowances from one of the princely houses. Prize money, available to Company surgeons, as they held commissions, were a further income source that could amount to as much as Rs 22,478 or 11,239 for a surgeon or assistant surgeon respectively at the 'battle of Bijaigarh'.[8] Medicos could also, like Chevers' 'Philosophic Surgeon', 'frankly and unashamedly indulge in trade', in the highly lucrative manufacture of indigo or other profitable activities.[9]

No other income source was more disapproved of and likely to incite distrust in medicos' professional motives than the exploitation of hospital contracts. Until 1815 (in Bengal, and 1827 and 1828 in Madras and Bombay respectively) it was usually part of the regimental surgeon's duty to provide food, liquors, bedding, clothing and certain medicines for patients under his charge. The temptation to over-economize, to the detriment of the sick, was resisted by few medical officers. In the 1836 edition of the *India Journal of Medical and Physical Science* the story was related that in 'Lord Lake's camp such were the enormous receipts in consequence of these contracts for supplying corps with medicine, diet, and dhoolees, that Doctors Monroe and Cockrane especially realised the largest fortunes ever made in this country'.[10]

Many more charges of this sort were made – usually not without some overtone of admiration. A Joseph Hume (with an M.D. from St Andrews), for example, had come to India in 1797 in search of a fortune and had obtained the position of assistant surgeon in 1799. After about two decades in the Company's employ he resigned in 1818 with £40,000 – a sum he could never have made from medical practice alone. He subsequently sat in Parliament as an 'advanced Radical', held several prestigious positions (including the lord rectorship of Marishal College, Aberdeen, examiner of candidates for the Company's medical service and personal physician to the Duke of Wellington) and apparently devoted his leisure time to the task of translating Dante's *Inferno*.[11]

Large-scale embezzlement and earnings from hospital contracts were endemic among the medical profession in India. Asylum owners and superintendents were not immune. Valentine Conolly in Madras was perhaps the most successful. He established and owned the local lunatic asylum and also acted as its medical superintendent (with questionable zeal). He simultaneously was an influential member of the very medical board supposed to thwart corrupt practices. His successors, surgeons Fitzgerald and Dalton also gained reasonable prosperity. They had bought the asylum building together with the charge of the lunatics for a price three times above the premises' estimated value, and still realized considerable profit after just a few years. This kind of practice had been condemned by the general public and medical officers in England and was prohibited by the Company from 1823 onwards.[12] The East India Company, once alerted, strongly disapproved of the practice of trading in asylums and the Madras government consequently passed orders disallowing it.

In the middle of the nineteenth century members of the medical profession were apparently not always in favour of such profiteering. Forbes Winslow, editor of the *Journal of Psychological Medicine* and president of the association of medical officers of asylums and hospitals for the insane in England' (who himself owned two private lunatic asylums in London), complained in 1858 that asylums and their inmates could be 'brought into the market and offered for sale, like a flock of sheep, to the highest bidder'.[13] The sale, he asserted, was undertaken 'in a manner calculated to destroy all public confidence and trust, in the honesty, integrity, and even common respectability of those connected with similar institutions'. Private madhouse proprietors would not always be what John Conolly in 1830 called 'respectable, well-educated and humane individuals'. Often they had a lower-class background, not considered conducive to kindness and humanity towards their charges. 'The patients are transmitted', Conolly asserted, 'like stock in trade, from one member of the family to another, and from one generation to another; they come in youth to the father, they linger out their age with the son'.[14]

Similarly, the medical board of Bengal in 1836 inveighed against the continued existence of 'Beardsmore's Bedlam'. Beardsmore was no medical doctor, having previously served as a soldier. He was described by the board's medical officers as 'an industrious but uneducated man' who 'pretended to no medical knowledge, [who] has never claimed the merit of originating any sort of improvement'.[15] The tug-of-war between medical board and private madhouse owner went public several times, as Beardsmore tried to stop his business being jeopardized. He had 'no other means of subsistence but what he derive[d] from superintending' his private asylum.[16] The province's most influential medicos for their part declared that Beardsmore should at least be made to recognize that he was their 'subordinate' and preferably be stripped of the charge of public patients altogether.

The very fact that a medically unqualified, lower-class individual was allowed by the Company's authorities to manage an institution, was a challenge to the medical board's authority. J. Sawers, the board's secretary, asserted as early as 1820, dryly and with the acerbic calmness of those confident in their own superiority: 'I disapprove of your Institution altogether, Sir'.[17] He did his utmost to make life difficult for Beardsmore by attempting to reclassify patients and demanding changes in the prevailing staff structure. Sawers certainly nurtured a personal grudge against Beardsmore. His own private madhouse had been declared to be a 'damp, sultry and gloomy place', beyond repair,[18] notwithstanding his assertion that it was 'a very dry and comfortable habitation'.[19] Government had decided to have all public patients removed from there to be eventually transferred into the private asylum of one Beardsmore and a surgeon Robinson.

Despite these personal undercurrents, the 'Beardsmore affair' was a manifestation of a more general concern among the medical profession of the period. The members of the medical board feared that their authority as experts and their role as gatekeepers in matters medical might be undermined by interlopers such as Beardsmore. They claimed that the involvement of the laity in the private 'mad-business' would bring the medical profession into disrepute. In short, the medical board of Bengal as much as Winslow in England and many other asylum superintendents were anxious lest 'guilt by association' adversely affect the medical professionals' still fragile reputation and status.

In India practitioners' fear of being tainted by avaricious medicos of doubtful expertise became widespread once the Company took the first steps to check its employees' pursuits of profit from non-medical or corrupt activities and had more clearly formulated the standards of formal and practical qualification required on entry to the medical services. In 1826 officers in the Bengal army, for example, were forbidden to engage in commercial speculation (whilst those in civil employ were, until 1841, left to make the most of the East's bounty). Commissioned Company servants were in general paid relatively generous salaries, and from 1842 received increased pensions. Medical staff were also required to be at least qualified in the practice of the healing arts. From 1822, candidates had to produce a diploma from one of the Royal Colleges of Surgeons (of London, Dublin or Edinburgh) or the College and University or the Faculty of Physicians and Surgeons of Glasgow. They were also required to undergo examination by the Company's physician in London, to attend a course of lectures in 'Hindoostanee' and, from 1828 onwards, were advised to take with them to India a copy of J. Annesley's pioneering reference book *Researches into the causes, nature and treatment of the more prevalent diseases of India.*[20] Medical service in India was becoming a professional career rather than a scramble for wealth. The introduction of competitive exams in 1855 set the seal on this process.

Towards the middle of the century, the Company's policy of discouraging corruption and mediocre medical practice by paying handsome salaries, granting pensions and tightening standards for entry into the medical service certainly had led to better qualified and more reliable medical servants applying for positions in the East. Misappropriation of hospital funds occurred less frequently and the quality of patient care, and with it of Company doctors' reputation, seem to have risen slowly. Medical officers in India themselves played an important part in this process. They founded their own professional lobbies in order to assert their expertise and knowledge and to defend their interests against 'interlopers' (especially against those without formal medical training or practising in one of the classical Indian traditions such as *yunani* and *ayurveda*).[21]

There existed as yet no organized interest group lobbying for those engaged in the management and treatment of the mad in India (such as the association of asylum superintendents in England). Neither 'asylum science' nor the treatment of the mad were amongst the subjects with which candidates for the medical service had to be familiar.[22] Lunatic asylums were usually only one amongst many of an assistant surgeon's (and, rarely, of a surgeon's) charges. Towards the middle of the century – when asylums had grown bigger – a medical officer's other duties were more restricted and he spent more time within the asylum. But, still he usually held the office of asylum superintendent for only a short period. W. Campbell, superintendent of the Bombay asylum for about 15 years, was certainly an exception. Once a medico was promoted he would relinquish his former tasks and a new officer would take his place. On average he would be in charge for only about two years before he was promoted to a better paid and more reputable position. One consequence of

Figure 7. Naval Hospital, Madras, 1811.

such high staff turnover in asylums was that superintendents found it hard to take much interest in the part of their duty that still carried with it so many negative connotations. Acting superintendents tended to confine themselves to carrying out the minimum required, leaving the day-to-day management of the place to their subordinates, especially when the premises themselves were in a state of dilapidation.

Lack of specialization and high staff turnover were not confined to the lunacy-sector. The scope of any Company medico's duties was in general very different from that of a medical officer working in Britain. In 1841 J. M'Cosh, former graduate of the Royal College of Surgeons, Edinburgh and lecturer in clinical medicine at the New Medical College, Calcutta, highlighted some of the peculiarities of service under the Company in his *Medical Advice to the Indian Stranger*. 'In India, no distinction is made', he said, 'between the practice of medicine and surgery'.[23] Consequently, 'every officer must act in either capacity, as circumstances demand', and must be willing to 'exercise his profession in the most comprehensive sense of the word'. In Europe, on the other hand, specialization in a particular branch of medicine or surgery (and, eventually, in psychiatry) had become increasingly common. Such specialization often constituted the necessary precondition for a medico's rise to fame and wealth. This was not yet the case for the ordinary Company doctor.

When medical officers in India did gain a reputation for specialized expertise, it was more often in the domain of biology, ethnology or linguistic skills than in the subject of medicine or surgery. Many early nineteenth-century doctors were keen travellers and collectors of plants and artefacts. A few even wrote dictionaries of Indian languages or published illustrated accounts of tribal customs. Such leisurely pursuits helped to counteract those 'dangers of ennuie and hypochondriasis' to which Dr M'Cosh expressly alerted the 'Indian Stranger'.[24] They fitted the public image of a surgeon's task in the East. He was not only expected to engage in his 'more regular duties', but 'as occasion presents itself should 'act the part of aurist, oculist, accoucheur, chemist, and medical jurist'. 'But this is not enough', warned M'Cosh the unwary newcomer,

> he ought to be able to physic his own horse or dog, superintend the construction of his own house, or boat, or baggage-waggon, know how to grow green-peas and cauliflowers, how to fatten capons and sucking-pigs, how to make jug-soup and tapioca, how to shoot wild-geese, ride a steeple-chase, drive a cabriolet, and sail a cutter, how to balance the debtor and creditor side of his monthly-accounts to the utmost farthing, how to calculate half-batta in vulgar and decimal fractions, and how to argue, logically, against retrenchments.[25]

The early part of the nineteenth century was the period when the medical profession began to flex its muscles and assert its professional authority – in British India and in Britain. In regard to what later came to be labelled 'psychiatry', however, the process of medical professionalization in British India lagged behind developments in Europe. Madness had certainly become medicalized in that the European insane were subject to medical attention rather than being simply left to the charge of the police authorities. (Unlike the Indian mentally ill, the European insane would rarely be looked after by their own relatives who were, in most cases, back home in Britain. Nor were Europeans cared for by missionaries, as in German colonial territories in Africa toward the beginning of the twentieth century.) Company surgeons came in a variety of guises, with different social backgrounds, qualifications, ambitions and approaches. The care of the insane impacted on their other commitments to differing extents.

For example, contrast the basis of surgeon Valentine Conolly's reputation with that of surgeon Cantor. Conolly belonged to the 'old breed' of Company servants who came to India in search of fortune, found it and returned home to Britain to enjoy their retirement in ease and luxury. They rarely excelled in anything strictly professional, being remembered rather for those activities that gained them their wealth (in Conolly's case, the establishment of Madras's first madhouse). Cantor was completely different. He took up medical practice as a career in itself rather than merely as a conduit to trade and speculation. He was regarded by his colleagues as a competent practitioner. He had been superintendent of the lunatic asylum in Penang, had published a report on his work there and was, on transfer to India, entrusted with re-organizing the hitherto privately managed Calcutta lunatic asylum. He also superintended and reformed the 'native' lunatic asylum in Dullunda. Cantor was not unaware of his prominent position as the province's first, officially acknowledged expert in lunacy. He proudly cited his experience in South East Asia and frequently referred knowledgeably to asylum management as practised in England and France, though never failing to point out that circumstances in India demanded some modification of treatment principles.

What made the career of Conolly and that of Cantor so different was that the former had established his fame when becoming a 'nabob' was still seen as a normal and legitimate aspiration. Cantor, in contrast, took up practice in the East when the standards of his profession and those of the East India Company demanded that medical officers should be reasonably well qualified and should devote their time and energy primarily to their medical duties. However, although Conolly and Cantor may be juxtaposed as ideal examples of the gradual shift from pecuniary gain to the beginnings of medical professionalization, there are also examples of asylum doctors who would not readily fit into this dichotomy. The world of medical practice was as yet neither ordered nor standardized. Surgeon Dick, for example, owned a madhouse in Bengal around the time Conolly left Madras. Dick was a successful entrepreneur in the 'mad-business'. Yet he was equally adept as a medical doctor. Back in England he assured himself of various reputable medical appointments and even became examiner of the Company's candidates for the medical service.

On the other hand, one of Cantor's contemporaries in Bombay failed to gain official recognition as a specialist in lunacy – despite his determined efforts to convince the provincial medical and government authorities of his expertise. Surgeon W. Campbell was asylum superintendent from 1849 to 1864 and was greatly devoted to the care of his European patients. He undoubtedly saw himself as an expert on insanity. His approach was broadly based upon principles of 'moral therapy', but he recognized the need for specialist training and consequently suggested that he be sent to Europe to make himself familiar with the most modern principles of asylum management and psychological medicine. His request was however declined and he pottered on in the Bombay asylum as a mad-doctor. Campbell had made the mistake of specializing in a marginalised area of medicine before he had consolidated his position as a practitioner in general (and before he had made friends among the more influential individuals of Bombay's professional bodies).

Dr W. Arbuckle, who preceded him in the charge of the Bombay lunatic asylum, had a completely different understanding of what asylum superintendence would entail for his career. Arbuckle had himself elected onto various professional bodies, such as the Medical and Physical Society of Bombay. The superintendency of the Bombay lunatic asylum was for him only one, instrumental, step in his career. He was familiar with the mainstream ideas in the treatment of the insane, but he subscribed to a more narrowly medical model. This fitted in well with his general ambitions as one of the town's most renowned medical practitioners. The professional kudos that could be gained was, so it seems, very much dependent on the particular branch of medicine a doctor was in, and the superintendence of madhouses was not a position that would necessarily ensure a rise in social and professional status.

The Medicalization of Madness

The impression that emerges from an examination of various asylum superintendents' careers over the first half of the nineteenth century is not only one of increasing professionalization, but also of a process of the medicalization of madness. However, doctors were not yet fully successful in establishing with the Company's authorities in India the necessity of an exclusively medical authority in the management of the mad. It has already been noted that the lunatic asylum in Calcutta had been owned and managed by a non-medico for more than three decades (despite repeated protests by the local medical authorities). When in 1856 Dr J. Cantor was finally authorized to take over the Beardsmores' asylum, the seal of medical supremacy in the treatment of the insane in British India's main centres was set. However, the care for the mentally ill only gradually became universally acknowledged as an area of medical science requiring specialist skills. Cantor's appointment could nevertheless be seen to mark a movement away from the conviction that the care of the mad was merely a 'difficult' and 'peculiar' task, to the opinion that the mentally ill could only be looked after by specialists with broad medical qualifications.

Contrasting assessments of the state of the art towards the second half of the nineteenth century point to a lack of professional unanimity. J. C. Bucknill and D. H. Tuke, authors of the *Manual of Psychological Medicine*, asserted optimistically in 1858 that 'a knowledge of the nature and treatment of Insanity is now expected of every well-educated man'.[26] On a more realistic note, J. M. Granville, the author of *The Care and Cure of the Insane*, still held in 1877 that the 'lack of acquaintance with lunacy is extraordinary. The great body of medical men appear to know scarcely more of arrangements and methods of treatment adopted in asylums than the general public'.[27]

The process of medicalization was slowed down by the emergence of the new paradigm of 'moral therapy'. This approach was based on the assumption that the insane were essentially human though lacking in self-control and discipline. By substituting physical restraint and punishment by kindness and moral education, the Tukes, the main protagonists of moral therapy in Britain, had achieved great fame. Most pertinently, however, the Tukes' humane, if paternalistic, mode of treatment was fuelled by their Quakerism rather than by any medical expertise. Their success in the treatment of fellow Quakers in the York Retreat constituted, as Bynum has pointed out, a 'damning attack on the medical profession's capacity to deal with mental illness'.[28] The Tukes' regime could produce high recovery rates, whilst the medical profession had hardly any comparable achievements to show. Similarly, G. Higgins (a magistrate in York who was instrumental in uncovering abuse of inmates in the local asylum and who contributed to a significant decrease in patients' deaths by helping to establish a system of lay visitations and public control) asserted that hardly anybody could doubt the superior efficacy of the peculiar 'medicine' advocated by him, namely 'visitors and committees'. He made the challenging claim that public supervision of asylum affairs alone would do more than, for example, 'Dr Hunter's famous secret *insane powders* – either green or grey – or his patent Brazil salts'.[29]

Doctors themselves had to admit that medicine's success in treating insanity was restricted. Dr Thomas Monro, an acknowledged expert in the medical treatment of the insane as physician to Bethlem Hospital, conceded before the select committee on the better regulation of madhouses in England in 1815 that insanity 'is not cured by medicine'.[30] The important point that had emerged in England at the beginning of the nineteenth century was that, as Bynum aptly put it, 'if physicians *qua* physician could do nothing for the lunatic except treat his bodily afflictions, then the medical man had no special claim to a unique place in the treatment of mental illness'.[31] As a consequence, doctors' 'income, prestige, and medical theories were all threatened'.

The medical profession in British India was in principle faced with these same dilemmas. The idea of 'moral therapy' and the news of the Tukes' success in treating the insane almost without restraint or recourse to medical nostrums, reached the British community in India towards the turn of the century. The provinces' medical boards responded by asserting that whilst kindness and humanity were essential in the management of the mad, lack of medical expertise would have harmful effects. After all, insanity was believed to be a disease of the brain. The claim that madness was in the last instance somatic, seemed to justify medical dominance in the treatment of its sufferers. Practitioners chose to reconcile the non-medical dogma of humane and kind treatment with their interest in 'income, prestige, and medical theories' by acknowledging the partial importance of 'moral therapy', whilst strongly rejecting the notion that 'management did more than medicine'.[32] This is highlighted by the Bengal medical board's allegations against Beardsmore, whose 'plan of moral treatment' it considered inadequate in that it lacked the 'intimate and…cultivated experience of the varied forms and shades of mental disease as well as a more enlarged philanthropy' so 'indispensable' in asylum management. It was also 'unaided and uncontrolled by the Ordinary medical Attendant'.[33] When in 1855 the board's submission that it was 'on the whole advisable to dispense with' the asylum owner's services was accepted by the government, the medical profession had at last succeeded in asserting its authority.[34]

The Subordination of 'Native' Medicine

Company surgeons' rise to professional authority was fraught with obstacles and endless struggles for power, as evidenced by the almost continual dispute between Beardsmore and the Bengal medical board. Colonial medical experts' competitive spirit and social and racial snobbery tended to get provoked still further by the fact that the European ruling elite had established itself as superior to those it regarded as its native colonial subjects. The European community in general had developed a distaste for people of Indian and mixed race. Doctors were not free from such prejudice. Company surgeons frequently expressed their unease at the presence of a great number of non-Europeans in the Indian medical department.

They in fact had ample scope for venting their racial sentiments, as Eurasians, for example, would usually be assigned to every European regiment as apothecaries and stewards, working under a European surgeon. In some cases Europeans, too, took up such positions. But they were usually 'the sons of sergeants or soldiers, who have not had the advantage of a European education'.[35] In view of their lower-class background and deprived of the supposed blessings of a British education, they too would be almost exclusively relegated to subordinate positions. Indian practitioners or 'native doctors' however got the worst of racial and social discrimination. They were permitted to take up only a restricted range of very inferior positions in the Company's employ and usually worked as assistants to European medical officers in charge of 'native troops', hospitals or jails.

Medical practices based on the eminent classical traditions of the Hindu (ayurveda) and Islamic (yunani) healing arts, of course, continued to be relevant to the majority of people in India. So were medical traditions practised by healers, such as fakirs, *maulanas*, *ojhas*, *pujaris* and *pandits*, that were usually derogatively described by the Western as well as the ayurvedic and yunani medical communities as 'folk medicine'. Among the European community, any other than 'modern' European medical practice was regarded with contempt.

Although banished to the lower orders of medical practice, subordinate members of the Company's medical department still posed a potential threat to a professional clique eager to consolidate its own, still precarious position. Even those medical officers who were convinced of the unquestionable superiority of European medicine had to concede (not without derogatory asides) that 'some medicines' prescribed by Indian practitioners work with 'great efficacy' and that they were administered 'occasionally with success' and that operations were practised 'with more skill than from their very rude instruments could be anticipated'.[36] Even in regard to the method of Indian inoculation, disparaged by the authorities, some European medicos admitted that 'not more than one percent die' in consequence of its application.

The acknowledgement (however reluctant and circumspect) that indigenous medicine could often be successful tended to fuel the ever-growing hostility towards them. The fierceness with which the campaign against all Eastern healing systems was fought during the 1830s by the majority of European medical practitioners can partly be accounted for by an underlying feeling of threat and the awareness of Western medicine's relative impotence in the face of high disease and mortality rates. The dominance of European medicine was asserted, symbolically as much as practically, by having the formal mainstays of organized medical practice in British India, namely the provinces' medical schools, transformed into training schools on a par with colleges in Britain. In Calcutta, for example, where indigenous as well as Western medicine was taught at the Sanskrit College and the Madrassa, lectures in Urdu were scrapped and students were instructed in English in anatomy, chemistry, surgery, *materia-medica*, physics and practical dissection by professors trained in Britain.

Despite these efforts to 'spread the light of European knowledge and civilization' among 'native' and Eurasian candidates for the medical service, suspicion as to the new converts' loyalty to Western ways was widespread. J. M'Cosh, who had lectured in clinical medicine at the *new* medical college in Calcutta, exclaimed, for example, in 1841 that he was 'inclined to think very favourably' of his students' 'zeal, of their capacity, and of their attainments'.[37] Yet he added, that his

> only fears were, that the want of integrity, so general in the Native character, would, notwithstanding their enlightened education, still cling to them as their birthright; and that, on any trying emergency, or dangerous personal illness, they would distrust their European doctrines, and resort to their national empyricism, or to superstitious invocation of the deities of their fathers.

The colonialist's task was, it seems, not an easy one. Medical officers were not to be spared the disappointment of those very pupils, who had been ridded of a 'mere combination of quackery and superstition' by laboriously imparted Western knowledge, easily reverting to their 'native ways'.[38] The mere conviction that Western medicine was best, was in a colonial setting sufficient to forcefully (and in the opinion of the European rulers, legitimately) establish its supremacy. The gradual marginalization of Eurasian and Indian practitioners and their subordination to Western medical practices was one component of this process.

Advancing European medicine of course also pervaded British India's madhouses. In these specialized institutions change was discernible, although the medical treatment and the general management of the insane were but tangentially affected. After all, the responsibility for European patients had always been with a European superintendent. Only in 'native lunatic asylums' were Indian assistants customarily entrusted with the day-to-day care of Indian and lower-class Eurasian patients. But even there a European had always been authorized to control the treatment of the Indian insane. A general order of 1826 expressly stipulated that 'Half-castes and other natives...be confined to subordinate offices'.[39] Ever since the establishment of lunatic asylums in India it had been difficult to attract reliable European employees. In consequence of the new, race-specific regulation, asylum superintendents found it even more difficult to enlist, for example, apothecaries who were racially acceptable as well as suitable for their task in terms of their character, qualification and experience. Subordinate staff and in particular asylum keepers or attendants were extremely poorly paid and work in a *pagal-khana* or madhouse did not appeal to many.

As in Britain, those attending on the mentally ill would frequently be 'such as are unable to obtain places elsewhere' or, as Scull put it, be drawn from 'the dregs of society'.[40] Staff turnover rates were high, superintendents' complaints numerous and the government authorities' displeasure with subordinate medical staff's and keepers' unreliability evident. Despite problems in inducing Europeans or Eurasians 'of a respectable class' to take up subordinate positions in the provincial capitals' asylums, the Company did not even consider changing its recruitment policy. Indians were excluded, no matter how badly equipped European and Eurasian aspirant apothecaries, overseers, stewards and matrons were for their job.

Although asylum staff were considered by protagonists of 'moral therapy' to be 'most essential instruments', superintendents were primarily concerned with establishing that expert medical management dominated the treatment of the insane.[41] Medical officers would, of course, insist (albeit mostly unsuccessfully) that they be authorized to employ a sufficient number of staff in order to guarantee the security and day-to-day care of patients. At the same time they preferred to pass on orders to European and Eurasian staff of inferior abilities and of doubtful character, rather than supervising Indian employees.

Hierarchical regulation of employment such as that introduced by surgeon Cantor in Calcutta rendered the lower strata 'native establishment' almost as subordinate to the whims of their European superiors and the constraints of a hierarchically structured institution as the patients they were supposed to care for. It appears then that, although, in general, problems in the recruitment and management of subordinate staff similar to those that prevailed in the majority of asylums in Britain were also present in India, racial discrimination specific to the European asylum in colonial India exacerbated the staff problems.

Medicine and Empire

Associated with the colonial setting was the peculiar career structure of officers in the Indian medical service. The most crucial difference from that of medical practitioners in Britain was that medical men in India automatically held a commission when joining the service. They would usually enter employment with the Company as ensign (or lieutenant) *and* assistant surgeon. When promoted they had to decide in which branch to continue their career, but were in any case subject to recall to military duty. Changes of position and re-appointments occurred frequently. These were occasioned mainly by the high fatality rate among Company servants and fluctuating manpower demand arising from the engagement of the Company's European army in various wars and 'punitive expeditions' during the earlier part of the nineteenth century. Medical officers in India consequently had much less freedom in deciding where to practise than their colleagues in Britain. They also did not have the possibility of opting out of assignment to any specific regiment when they found the duties and lifestyle unpalatable.

The strong link between medicine and the military in India had implications that went far beyond individual doctors' discomfiture. It also serves, as Arnold pointed out, 'as a reminder of the enduring importance of the army within the British colonial system in India', and, what is more, underlines the fact that the doctor 'who practised among the European soldiery...bore a formidable responsibility for the maintenance of British military power in India'.[42]

What concerned the medical officers newly arrived from England most, was the immediate practical and mundane implications of their 'formidable responsibility'. If they were lucky they would not straight away have to face up to the full range of professional tasks of a civil surgeon or regimental doctor and to the unfamiliar duties that, according to Dr M'Cosh, life in the East demanded. If there was no urgent need associated with epidemic or warfare, the newly commissioned assistant surgeon would spend a couple of months at one of the general hospitals acclimatizing himself to the formal requirements of his new position and getting habituated to 'the diseases peculiar to the country, and the treatment put in practice'.[43] The chance of becoming familiar with the more ubiquitous diseases afflicting the town's European citizens was however at

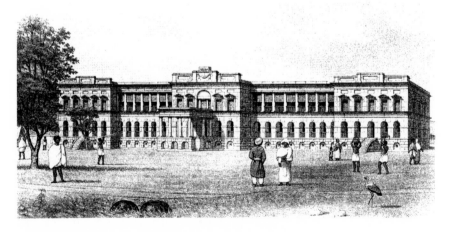

Figure 8. The New General Hospital, Calcutta, 1829.

times somewhat restricted. The general hospital in Calcutta, for example, practised a socially and racially discriminatory admissions policy via high charges. This reduced its usefulness for the general European public and its scope as a training school.

The young assistant would nevertheless soon pick up general custom and practice. Being initiated into the Company's medical service (regardless of which branch) implied that the trainee had to 'consider himself in the vortex of Indian society'.[44] 'Indian' society was here meant to refer to the ways peculiar to both the European expatriate and the indigenous communities. A newcomer was therefore required to 'conform to the manners and customs of his compatriots' and expected to 'submit to the numerous prejudices of caste among the Natives, and be contented'. He was to be 'constantly upon his guard against anger, for he will have much to irritate him'. And 'on no account' was he to 'give way to beating his servants, a practice too common amongst new-comers'. Old India hands themselves rarely lived up to these imperatives.

India was for many 'a dreadfully difficult country' and its strange ways and customs (both Indian and European) were a trial for the uninitiated and faint of heart.[45] This was true as much for the officer and civil servant as for the soldier and sailor, for the doctor as much as for the patient in the madhouse. Moreover, disease would hit the medico as badly as it affected his officer-colleagues whose privileges, lifestyle and habits he shared. The 'cloud of melancholy' could hover over the tent or compound of the surgeon as thickly as over his patients'. The fact that disease and even madness struck the very experts who were supposed to maintain the health and sanity of others tended to strengthen the belief among civilians and soldiers that the preservation of one's health in the tropics was dependent on 'God's providence' or the preventive powers of alcoholic spirits, tobacco, exercise, warm clothing and devices such as the 'cholera belt' rather than on medical expertise.

Moreover, European doctors generally lacked the means and skills necessary to ameliorate the condition of what a royal commission called the 'sickly army in India'.[46] European medical science was in the early nineteenth century not yet in a position to boast much success in the cure of the most common diseases among Europeans in India. Nor were its methods of pain relief and of symptomatic treatment very effective. It is true that the discovery of a vaccine against smallpox, for example, helped to reduce the number of fatalities from a disease that had been endemic in certain parts of India. The disdain bestowed on Indian *tikadars* (who had for centuries performed inoculation against smallpox) by Company authorities and the public at large certainly confirm that by the 1830s European science and medicine had come to be perceived as the paragon of knowledge and civilization. J. R. Martin voiced in 1835 a widespread conviction when he exclaimed that the diffusion of European medical science, with its collateral branches, must prove one of the most direct and impressive modes of demonstrating to the natives, the superiority of European knowledge in general, and that they must cultivate it actively if they would rise in the scale of nations.[47]

However, despite the zeal occasionally exhibited to eradicate 'superstition' and 'bigotry' in Indian medical systems and the success of vaccination campaigns among Europeans, Western medicine performed poorly during the Company's Raj in India. Cholera, which accounted between 1830 and 1846 for about ten per cent of deaths among the British in Bombay[48] and between 1818 and 1854 killed more than 8,500 British soldiers[49], was not for decades to be successfully checked. Similarly the hazards of 'fevers' and 'dysentry and diarrhoea' that killed on average about one quarter and one third of the sick, respectively, were to be ameliorated only towards the beginning of the twentieth century. The health of army servants in particular was notoriously bad during the early decades, with a mortality rate from disease seven times higher than that from wartime casualties. Soldiers would maintain that it was in most cases 'disease, and not the enemy that killed' their comrades.[50] Against the various forms of madness medical doctors could do little but help to ease patients' physical condition and refer Europeans to the care of practitioners in England.

The extremely bad state of health of army personnel in India – even by the middle of the century mortality rates were over double those among the military in Britain – was not entirely to be blamed on a failure of European medicine. Nor did there exist any effective medicine that would cure insanity. Death was more common among the lower ranks and was closely linked with unsanitary and cheerless living conditions, inadequate diet and abuse of the liquor bottle. The question of life and death was consequently not one that could be dealt with by a medical practitioner alone. This was acknowledged and indeed emphasized by the royal commission on the sanitary state of the army in India in their summary statement:

> it is necessary to bear in mind that the soldier's health in India, as elsewhere, is the product of all the conditions to which he is exposed. It is not solely the result of climate, nor of locality and dwelling place, nor of diet, habits, nor duties; it is the product of all of these.[51]

Despite the admission that a combination of factors would affect 'the soldier's health' and the fact that medical officers would see many more of their patients die than they could restore to health, the role of the doctor was perceived by the Company's authorities to be indispensable. Medicine and its practitioners gradually gained prestige and status at a period and in circumstances when the medical profession was (in terms of cure rates and symptomatic and pain relief) not particularly successful in the practice of its trade. Considering therefore that medical officers in the East India Company's employ were faced with an enormous incidence of disease and with insalubrious and stressful living conditions, whilst lacking the drug technology of later decades that would have allowed for instant cures, they did not do badly in asserting their position as the ultimate authority in matters of healing.

It was above all during these early decades of the nineteenth century that the foundation for the enduring great colonial medical myth was laid. The medical doctor was to become a major pillar of European colonial ideology in that his services for the good of humankind were seen to legitimate foreign rule and to serve as proof of the unquestionable superiority of Western civilization. This conviction was expressed frequently (most succinctly by Martin in the 1830s) and even as recently as 1950, when D. MacDonald, a former member of the Indian Medical Service and author of *Surgeons Twoe and a Barber. Being Some Account of the Life and Work of the Indian Medical Service*, would place on the front page of his book Marshal Hubert Lyautey's epigram that 'the doctor is the sole excuse for colonization'.

Those who cared for the mentally ill in British India were not always medical doctors. When medical practitioners became professionalized and distanced themselves from the trade in sickness, medically trained asylum superintendents lagged behind, as they failed to convince government and medical authorities of their special professional skills. By mid-century, however, the medicalization of madness in India was all but complete, as Western expertise in the care of the sick in mind joined that of the sick in body as a significant component of the apparatus for imposing the enlightened nostrums of European civilization upon colonial India – at the expense of indigenous skills.

Chapter 5

THE PATIENTS

'Highly Irregular Conduct' and 'Neglect of Duty'

In early spring 1845, a young Indian Navy officer by the name of Edward Charles Z. was embarked on the *Imam of Muscat* on account of his deranged state of mind. Lieutenant Z. had been granted a sick certificate that entitled him to three years furlough in England. He had served on several of the Company's vessels in India since April 1830 and was put on the sicklist in July 1844 on return from a naval mission to the Persian Gulf. At that stage of his career the then 28 year-old was keen to see the last of duty in India and yearned to be allowed to proceed to Europe on sick leave. However, he was thwarted in this by Company authorities anxious not to worsen the navy's pressing manpower needs. Z. developed symptoms of 'mania' or, as the certifying doctor in Bombay put it, on the refusal of sick-leave 'his mental symptoms seem to have supervened'.[1]

Further investigation by a medical committee on the authenticity and severity of Z.'s mental symptoms revealed several earlier instances of odd behaviour recollected by fellow-officers. While on duty on one of the Company's receiving ships, for example, 'his Conduct had attracted the notice of every one on board'.[2] Not only did he walk 'the deck night, and day successively', but he also one morning 'fancied that he was to be hanged at eight o'clock' and 'attended punctually for the purpose and behaved in the most extravagant manner, when the hour passed and his anticipation had not been realized'. It emerged that Z. had 'always been considered by the officers of his own Service as being of unsound mind'. Many more corroborative events were related to the committee. One event in particular had created both amusement and bewilderment. On board ship, Z. had 'imagined himself transformed into a vegetable, an artichoke, and was in the habit of taking advantage of every shower, that fell in order that he might be properly watered'.

Lieutenant Z. was consequently seen as fit for the province's lunatic asylum and was, in September 1844, admitted to the institution on the Kolaba peninsula as a 'maniac with a melancholic trait'. After only a couple of months he was reported to have fallen into 'a state of confirmed idiocy'. In the absence of any significant improvement, Z. was finally recommended for transfer to Europe.

Apart from the charming artichoke episode, Z.'s case shares certain characteristics with several of his fellow inmates' in the asylum. Like him, a great number of the mad had previously suffered from various physical illnesses. They had frequently been subject to medical treatment, either (in the case of military or naval personnel) in one of the regimental or port hospitals or else (in the case of civilians or high-ranking officers) in the general hospital or at their own homes under the civil surgeon's professional attention.

Private Timothy C. of the second European regiment and formerly a labourer in Ireland was admitted to the Calcutta lunatic asylum in June 1841, suffering from 'mania periodica'.[3] A few months previously, in February, he had been admitted into the regimental hospital with 'febrile symptoms and a quick and hot pulse attended with delirium, having made an attempt to drown himself'. A year later, in August 1842, gunner Patrick L., formerly a weaver of Cork, Ireland, joined the patients in the Calcutta second-class ward.[4] He too had a recent history of physical ailments. He had been admitted to the regimental hospital for pain in the back of the head, chronic hepatitis and 'symptomatic affections of the Intestines'. When 'symptoms of mental aberration' were observed, he was transferred to the province's madhouse. He was diagnosed as suffering from 'Theo Mania' due to his persistent 'delusion that he beheld visions and had conversations with the Allmighty'. At around the same time, in 1843, another Irishman, Private James B., was admitted to the asylum in Madras.[5] He, too, had been sent to his regiment's hospital some months previously when he suffered from delirium tremens, and subsequently from an attack of fever. And finally, Gunner Thomas H. of the Horse Artillery, having suffered 'two severe falls from his horse at riding drill', was treated in the local hospital and on presentation of mental symptoms was transferred to the lunatic asylum.[6]

Hospitalization on account of accidents, fever, syphilis, cholera, diarrhoea and delirium tremens was one experience commonly shared by most asylum inmates. Similarly common was inmates' previous experience of disciplinary punishment: verbal reprimand, downgrading in rank, tightened drill and solitary confinement. Only some five years before Lieutenant Z. had turned into a vegetable, he had been court-martialled in Bombay Harbour and reprimanded for 'most disgraceful and highly irregular conduct and neglect of duty to the prejudice of good order and naval discipline'.[7] Z., then a midshipman, was ordered to assume temporary charge of the Company's steam vessel *Atalanta* moored in Bombay Harbour and had failed to keep control of the situation when the ship had caught fire. Various other superior officers had rushed to the burning vessel and had taken over command from him. An argument ensued during which Z. had been accused by the other officers of being too drunk to perform his duty and that, apparently highly agitated, he was unable to manage the confusion on the burning ship.

For his superiors Z.'s behaviour was undoubtedly to be attributed to intoxication and he was censured as having been 'most disgraceful' and 'highly irregular'. Although Z. was eventually found not guilty of drunkenness by a court martial, the commander of the local forces and government strongly disapproved of 'both the verdict and the award'[8] and

> felt imperatively called on to counteract as far as possible, the serious evil that must result to the respectability, general efficiency, and well-being of the Indian Navy, were such an aggravated breach of duty, as is presented in the case under consideration, permitted to pass by unnoticed.[9]

The maintenance of discipline and the reputation of the service were given priority over both the process of the law and the compassion for which Z. pleaded in his defence speech. Z. was to be made an example of, given what was perceived to be 'the insubordinate and unmilitary feeling which prevails among many of the junior members of the Indian Navy'.

Undisciplined behaviour and neglect of duty could never be taken lightly by the military. Many a junior officer and soldier were subjected to the harsh consequences of military discipline. Z. suffered considerable social embarrassment in consequence of the *Atalanta* affair, although he was spared incarceration or prolonged suspension from duty. In many other cases, however, there were more adverse effects. Take the example of Daniel B., a 23 year-old gunner in the Madras artillery, who had attempted to stab his sergeant.[10] He was 'punished with solitary imprisonment', in consequence of which he became 'morose, suspicious, violent, and offensive in his language', so that admission to the lunatic asylum was seen to be indicated. Similarly, Private William W., a 24 year-old Englishman from Staffordshire, was on 13 April 1842

> pronounced to be of unsound mind by a Medical Board assembled at Trichinopoly in consequence of his having two days before, when a prisoner, attempted to strike a Sergeant with a steel fork, he having ordered him out for exercise when he was not inclined to go and after he had once refused.[11]

Officers who refused to carry out their duty or failed to submit to superiors' orders were sometimes treated more leniently. A Lieutenant J. H. H. of the Bengal native infantry apparently suffered from 'weak intellect', as he had shown 'much disinclination for the performance of duty and invariably reported unwell when the regiment was ordered for exercise'.[12] The regimental surgeon felt 'obliged to intimate to him that such a practice could not be permitted, and on his again absenting himself from parade without sufficient reason the Commanding Officer deemed it necessary to warn him of the consequences'. This official reprimand, 'together with the dislike to the performance of his duty', greatly affected H., but did not prevent him from absenting himself again when 'directed to put the Regiment through part of its exercise'. H. was finally to undergo examination by a medical committee. Although he did not have any mental symptoms and enjoyed very good general health, his refusal to attend to his business as an officer made him 'totally unfit for the performance of duty'. H. was pronounced 'imbecile' and sent to England 'to be placed under charge of his friends'.

For many the madhouse marked the endpoint of disciplinary measures. Particularly for the 'other ranks' any deviancy from the norm was seen as inexcusable and wilful disobedience. Only when the usual disciplinary actions had failed or when measures such as solitary confinement occasioned the breakdown of prisoners' state of mental health would punishment be substituted by treatment in the madhouse. Officers usually fared slightly better. Their breaches of discipline were met by the more 'temperate' responses due to persons of some social standing. Being pronounced 'insane' or 'imbecile' seems sometimes to have been preferred to the verdict of a court martial. Some allegedly 'mad' officers escaped the due process of the law by rendering themselves willing subjects of medical attention. The most blatant case was that of J. D. O.

O., assistant magistrate and collector at Murshidabad, held a prestigious position in the Bengal civil service and had the backing of his well-connected father, J. W. J. O., formerly in service in Bengal and subsequently lecturer in 'arabick' at the East India Company's College at Haileybury. Therefore, when O. junior 'stabbed a Native' in October 1854, he did not have to stand trial. His violent crime was considered 'the result of temporary insanity',[13] which was arising from 'too strict attention to his studies increased by his anxiety respecting an approaching examination'.[14] O. was pronounced 'really insane and unfit to take his trial' in India.[15] He was sent back to England and delivered to his father's care 'perfectly restored to mental and bodily health'.[16] His father petitioned Her Majesty and the authorities in Britain to take no further action against his son, even requesting that his son be allowed to return to Bengal.

The necessary medical certificate was obtained from the famous Sir Ranald Martin. It attested to the temporary character of young O.'s mental problems. After having carefully perused the several documents relating to the former lunatic's physical and mental state, Martin concluded that 'he suffered much in health in India, from mental over exertion in office, and in the study of requirements for an examination at the same time'.[17] Martin pointed out that he 'likewise suffered about this time from low fever; and while under both the influences…was subjected to severe solar exposure'. 'Under these disturbing causes', Martin held, 'the brain became congested and delirium was the result'.

Whitehall (and the Company) acquiesced in the plea, noting that there was 'reasonable ground for supposing that the act of violence committed by Mr [O.] was the result of temporary insanity, from which he has now recovered'. It was not considered necessary to 'propose advising the Crown to take any proceedings against him in this country, and he will consequently be at liberty either to return to India, or to remain here unmolested according to his own discretion'.[18] In May 1857, Professor O. was finally informed that permission had been obtained for his son to return to the East Indies.[19]

Though the madhouse frequently signified the nadir of the common sailor's or soldier's military career in the East, it did not necessarily mean the same to officers in the service. Being sent back home on medical certificate was certainly not perceived as the zenith of a lieutenant's or captain's professional life either, but in some cases at least it ensured that his career and reputation would not be seriously affected. In the case of an officer, disciplinary action may entail the withdrawal of commission. This was generally dreaded, as it implied the loss of a steady income and a decline in social status. As Lieutenant Z. put it when appealing to the members of the court martial, a 'merciful construction' should be put on his action, as otherwise his prospects might be 'totally ruined' and his 'character blasted and destroyed'.[20]

The consequences of certification of unsoundness of mind seemed less drastic. Unlike common soldiers and sailors, officers could well return to duty when their furlough was over and any mental symptoms had vanished. Their episode as mental patients did not necessarily expose them to any significant social stigma or occupational disadvantages. Lieutenant Z. had after three and a half years furlough in England gone back to duty in India despite his previous transformation into an artichoke. O., too, was permitted to return to India in pursuit of his career as a civil servant only three years after he had 'stabbed a Native'.

'Drawn Very Much from the Same Class'

Notwithstanding some class-specific differences as to the social and occupational implications of medical certificates, inmates of the three provinces' European lunatic asylums could be described as a relatively homogeneous group. Confinement in the madhouse was in many cases merely one step in a sequence of institutionalization. Inmates had simply been transferred: typically from the military barrack, to the hospital, back to the barracks, to the prison, and so to the asylum. The bulk of European asylum patients (about 80 per cent) was made up of military servants. Out of the 15 European patients confined in the Bombay Asylum in 1851/2, 11 had been soldiers or sailors.[21] This fact tended to be a great equalizer. Most men were 'drawn very much from the same class, belonging generally to the same profession and united in a majority of instances by identity of interest, taste, and pursuits'.

Few civilians could be found in the European asylums in Madras, Bengal and Bombay. In 1801 two out of seven Europeans in the Madras asylum were civilians, in 1808 the number of civilians reached four in contrast to 12 military servants.[22] Between 1841 and 1847 the Bengal asylum confined only eight civilian in contrast to ten times as many (83) military Europeans.[23] In part, this was because the number of non-military Europeans in British India during the early part of the nineteenth century was about half that of military personnel. Shortly after the Indian Revolt, in 1861, there were only about 42,000 civilians as compared with about 84,000 military servants.[24] It was also the case that an asylum frequented by public patients was not always regarded by relatives as suitable for their dearest, however deranged. The very existence of Beardsmore's private lunatic asylum in Calcutta initially owed much to the apparent need 'to accommodate female Patients and others wishing to avoid public Exposure of a family misfortune'.[25] It also met the demand from those 'averse' to the idea of

> removing the relatives from their own immediate view to England where they have no connexions and to afford many other comforts, and conveniences which cannot be well expected or had at the public Hospital for Insanes.

From what is known, the few European civilians admitted to the government-controlled asylums in Calcutta, Madras and Bombay had no family connections in India, or their relatives were unable or unwilling to look after them at home. Some civilian patients had suffered loss, either of fortune as in the case of a Captain J. H., who endured a shipwreck in Penang in 1807, or of a close relative, as was the case with many of the European women received into the madhouse.[26] Mrs Joanna K. had come to India in 1835 with her husband James, formerly a labourer in Ireland and then gunner in the East India Company's service.[27] The couple had three young children when James K. died in 1841. As an army wife Mrs K. had little choice but to marry another man within the year in order to be allowed to stay on in India. This was required by army regulations designed to deter European single women from permanently 'joining' a regiment and pursuing 'immoral' and 'vicious' activities. Alternatively she could be sent back home to a Britain, hit by what Hobsbawm has aptly labelled 'waves of desperation' in the shape of social pauperization.[28]

Mrs K., in fact, chose neither to re-marry nor to return to a life of misery in Ireland, of which she was presumably glad to have seen the last just a decade earlier. From her husband's death she had been 'in a distressed state of mind' and, finally, on 1 January 1842, became 'so manifestly insane as to render it unsafe to leave her at large'.[29] She was first sent to the general hospital at Madras and after a couple more months was transferred to the lunatic asylum in a generally 'taciturn and dejected' condition. Mrs K. had meanwhile lost any 'interest in her children, to whom she previously appeared to be much attached'. The two boys and one girl were consequently sent to the Military Orphan Asylum in Madras. Mrs K. herself was sent to England where she remained in Pembroke House, suffering from 'dementia' until her death at the age of 78. According to the certifying doctor in Madras, though 'generally appearing to understand what is said to her', she never uttered 'more than a single word in reply'. By permanently withdrawing into herself, Mrs K. at least ensured that her beloved children would all be cared for somehow.

Personal bereavement was typical of other European women's life histories prior to confinement in the asylum. The prior history of male civilians was less homogeneous, although in their case, too, bereavement or loss of fortune were not uncommon. Such gender-specificity owes much to the relatively restricted options open to European women in the East; mainly that of wife or mother. Otherwise, they would be expected to live with their families rather than pursuing any independent trade or profession.

The cycle of hospital admission – back to duty – imprisonment – hospital admission – transfer to lunatic asylum…etc., frequently characterizing the personal history of military lunatics, was not typical of civilians. Civilians' asylum admission was often a result of the *lack* rather than the omnipresence of a supportive social network, or of an institutional authority controlling their behaviour and responsible for their care and security. However, the ubiquitous web of colonial administration did catch up with civilians at the magistrate's court. Lunatics who had behaved in a disorderly fashion in public were taken there by the police for certification. Those, whose physical state appeared to be at least as badly affected as their mind, would initially be recommended for admission to hospital for treatment and further observation. In many cases, however, certification at the court was followed by immediate confinement in the lunatic asylum.

A Passage from India

The European insane in India as a group possessed several special characteristics distinguishing them both from the insane in Britain and from the Eurasian mentally ill with whom they temporarily shared premises in India. Their predominantly military background and the practice of repatriation were largely responsible for this. Once Europeans finally arrived back home, the distinction seems to have blurred somewhat. First, it appears from the study of individual cases that some amongst them recovered on their passage from India. It is however as impossible to ascertain their exact number as it is to judge whether recovery was attributable to madness having been feigned, or to the tendency of mental illness sometimes to subside spontaneously.

Whatever the reason for such improvement, they would subsequently be reunited with their families or, in the case of the poor, take to the streets to sooner or later be picked up by the police and sent to the workhouse or back to the asylum. It was not uncommon for lunatics to be simply disembarked by the ship's captain on arrival in the first English port, regardless of their state of mind. In most cases, however, the new arrivals would be received into a lunatic asylum: many of them into Pembroke House, and the rest into a military or naval lunatic asylum or one of many prestigious private madhouses.

Like the inmates of Britain's early nineteenth-century madhouses, few mentally ill Europeans with previous Indian experience would normally end up in the institution for ever – notwithstanding exceptions such as Mrs K. For one thing, the cost of maintenance in the asylum was high in England and even higher in India. Europeans were therefore repatriated within a year and would in many cases remain in Pembroke House only until a relief of mental symptoms (rather than a perfect 'cure') occurred. The Company's authorities demanded regular returns from the proprietor of Pembroke House. In particular, the madhouse owner was obliged to assign reasons for every patient's confinement. This administrative control procedure did much to speed up discharges. Further, the belief in the curability of madness declined only slowly in the nineteenth century. Cures or relief of symptoms were therefore expected to occur, so that comparatively high discharge rates were common. Although re-admission rates, too, were high, confinement in an asylum did not as yet carry much threat of lifelong incarceration.

The slogan of 'no cure, no pay', spread by some private madhouse owners in England in order to attract clients, also helped to keep the length of stay down. That the privately owned Pembroke House enjoyed the patronage of the East India Company also had an impact. Such patronage seems to have been considered an obligation as much as a distinction. Dr G. Rees, the owner who had in 1818 entered into the agreement with the Company to receive its insane employees, even advertised his establishment in the following way:

> The high encomium which has been paid to the management of This Establishment, in the latest investigation into the state of Mad Houses by the House of Commons*, and the distinguished patronage of the HON. EAST-INDIA COMPANY, render it unnecessary to say any thing more in its favor. It will be sufficient therefore to add, that the number is limited, the Patients are select, the advantages are considerable, and the terms reasonable, and that *three-fourths of those already admitted have been restored to health and reason.*[30]

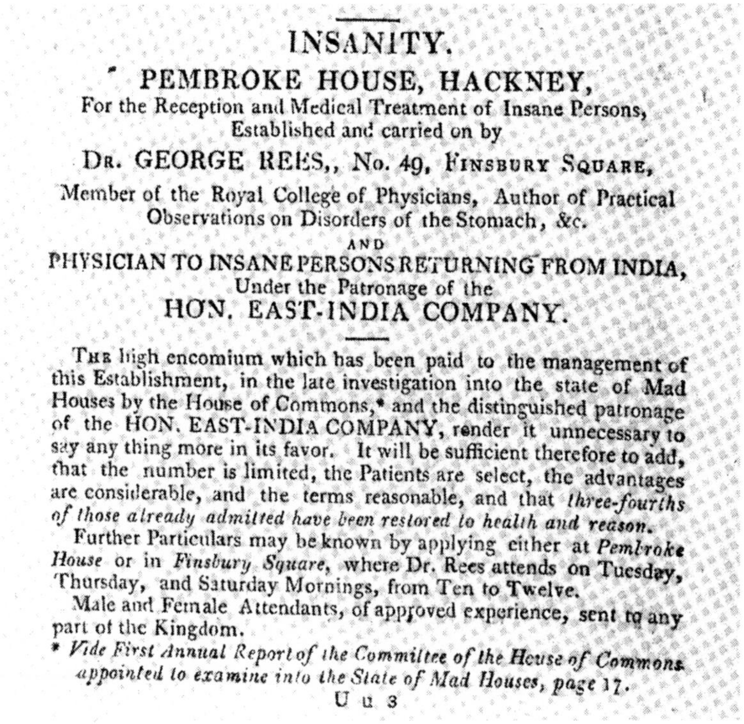

INSANITY,
PEMBROKE HOUSE, HACKNEY,
For the Reception and Medical Treatment of Insane Persons,
Established and carried on by
Dr. GEORGE REES,, No. 49, Finsbury Square,
Member of the Royal College of Physicians, Author of Practical
Observations on Disorders of the Stomach, &c.
AND
PHYSICIAN TO INSANE PERSONS RETURNING FROM INDIA,
Under the Patronage of the
HON. EAST-INDIA COMPANY.

The high encomium which has been paid to the management of
this Establishment, in the late investigation into the state of Mad
Houses by the House of Commons,* and the distinguished patronage
of the HON. EAST-INDIA COMPANY, render it unnecessary to
say any thing more in its favor. It will be sufficient therefore to add,
that the number is limited, the Patients are select, the advantages
are considerable, and the terms reasonable, and that *three-fourths
of those already admitted have been restored to health and reason.*
Further Particulars may be known by applying either at *Pembroke
House* or in *Finsbury Square*, where Dr. Rees attends on Tuesday,
Thursday, and Saturday Mornings, from Ten to Twelve.
Male and Female Attendants, of approved experience, sent to any
part of the Kingdom.
* *Vide First Annual Report of the Committee of the House of Commons
appointed to examine into the State of Mad Houses, page 17.*
U u 3

Figure 9. Advert of Pembroke House, Hackney, 1819.

The place's suitability for the upper classes, and in particular for those with Indian experience, thus seems to have been unquestioned. The integrity of its proprietor's motives and his expertise in caring for and curing the mentally ill seemed proven.

The Changing Fortunes of Asylum Inmates

Things changed over the decades in Pembroke House and in the European asylums in India. Patients' experience of asylum life not only varied greatly with their race and social position but also over time. Mrs N., who was admitted to Beardsmore's asylum in 1827, was a Eurasian lacking any independent financial means.[31] Her stay in the asylum was paid for by the Company and she was classified as a second-class patient. During the 1820s, 1830s and even 1840s she enjoyed exceptionally good conditions, as the asylum proprietor was then still intent on attracting private patients who might be deterred if the place gained a down-market reputation. In the 1850s, when a government investigation found that the upkeep of poor lunatics exhibited some 'extravagance', Mrs N.'s life was to change drastically. She was put on a parsimonious diet and was in general provided for at an inferior standard. By that time the premises had also become overcrowded and Mrs N. spent most of her time together with the many other women of mixed race, rather than with a majority of European women as she had done earlier.

In the first-class apartments institutional life was less obviously affected over the decades. G. S., a military officer, had been admitted to Beardsmore's asylum just two years before Mrs N., in 1825.[32] He, too, was born in India, the son of a European father and an Indian mother, and was therefore entitled to be sent to England for treatment. But on account of his officer status he was provided for as a first-class patient and was even allowed to take his food at the asylum proprietor's family table. He was allocated his own separate apartment, equipped with hanging lamps, washing facilities and other objects for daily use. He did not have to socialize with any of the 13 ward-patients who then lived in small and spartanly equipped cells in less comfortable buildings.

Some three and a half decades later, at the age of 76 and suffering from 'dementia', S. was still an in-patient. About 1,200 European and Eurasian patients had by then passed through the asylum and the average asylum population had increased to about 70 inmates, only eight of whom were first-class patients. Dining at the proprietor's family table together with other gentlemen and ladies was no longer encouraged once the place had become a public institution. The impact of changing times was however still much less on first-class patients such as S. than on the numerous second-class inmates who shared the ward with Mrs N.

Being Insane in British India

The question then arises of how the usual short-term and the less common long-term confinement in the Company's asylums in India and in Pembroke House were perceived by the inmates themselves. Only few and fragmentary accounts of patients' experiences exist and those that are available convey more in regard to a patient's relationship with a particular medical officer than about the general impact of life inside the asylum on inmates' state of mind. Gunner Francis H., for example, expressed his feeling of 'gratitude for the kindly interest' that he received from the superintendent.[33] H.'s state of mind greatly improved under his medical patron's charge. Confinement in the Bombay asylum must on the whole have been experienced by him as a welcome relief from the harsh life in the military that had become so unbearable.

Similarly, the medico who treated officer T., who apparently greatly disliked his father and mother, Colonel and Mrs T. of Baker Street, London, remarked that 'the most certain method of gaining his confidence is by treating him with respect'.[34] Lieutenant Z., the 'artichoke', too, seemed not at all ill-disposed to his confinement in the Bombay asylum. He was reported by his medical doctor to have taken pleasure in accompanying him 'regularly in a morning walk, taking great interest in the sea vessels and harbour'.[35] Z. recovered considerably in the Bombay asylum and, no further treatment in Pembroke House being indicated, enjoyed an extended furlough of three and a half years in England.

Even a man like gunner John T., admitted to the Madras asylum as a second-class patient in 1842 (labouring under the delusion of being 'Marquis of Anglesea and Viceroy of India, sometimes a Highland chieftain' or 'Colonel of the 15th Hussare', and frequently complaining of 'not receiving the luxuries suitable to his supposed rank'), soon became 'more cheerful than formerly' and was 'easily controlled without personal restraint, and merely required a purgative occasionally'.[36] On transfer back to England he stayed in Pembroke House for about three months and was subsequently allowed to live in '10 Horners Buildings', an almshouse in Southampton. From there he wrote to his former doctor at Pembroke House that he felt 'extremely obliged' to him for his 'care and attention'. John T. went on to confide that he was 'sorry to say' that he had 'no prospect at present of any situation' and hopefully asked if the doctor could 'confer a favour' on him by recommending him for any prospective employment.

Written evidence of patients' experience of life in asylums is particularly scarce for the lower classes. This is even more so in regard to soldiers who suffered from a short spell of mental derangement but were never admitted to the asylum. The number of those who were put on the sick list in their regiments on account of insanity appears to have been considerable. Some regimental statistics reveal a high incidence of such short-term cases but provide no further explanation as to the exact circumstances. What can be gleaned from the records is that temporarily insane soldiers were immediately on the relief of symptoms sent back on duty. The overall number of military personnel afflicted by insanity may have reached about 4 per cent of all hospital admissions.[37] Only between about 3 and 4 per cent of these died from what was considered to have been mental illness.[38] This low mortality rate may have greatly contributed to the fact that regimental medical officers concentrated their efforts on recording the medical histories of patients suffering from the more fatal diseases common among the soldiery in India rather than on the personal histories of patients who temporarily suffered from mental derangement.

One conclusion that can be drawn from the scarcity of patients' own accounts and of insufficient data on insanity in the barracks and civil lines is that the story of the inmates of the three provinces' European lunatic asylums and of Pembroke House is only partial and by no means typical of what it meant to be insane in British India. As pointed out by reformers and critics in more recent years who denounced institutional confinement as the incapacitation of the mad, the opinions, thoughts and feelings of the very people for whom specialized institutions had been established were in general (and apart from accounts of symptomatic behaviour) not considered medically relevant, nor important enough, to be officially recorded. Only in few instances were patients' own testimonies regarded as worth preserving. It was usually because of the intrinsic fascination of the story that the material was saved from oblivion. The perspective from which 'mad tales from the Raj' can be written is almost exclusively that of the Company's authorities and of the officers in the Indian medical service.

The general attitude that characterizes the situation was most aptly summarized by Dr W. Campbell of Bombay in 1852:

> The Records of an Asylum, if rightly read are fitted to teach us many touching, and instructive lessons. They tell us of disappointed love, blighted hope, and crushed ambition, of exhausting labour, distracting care, and corroding sorrow, of time mis-spent, and precious opportunities lost, or misapplied; of unbridled passion, un-resisted temptation; weakness, folly, dissipation, and crime.
>
> With the lessons they inculcate, however, or the moral they point, it is not our province to deal. We have to do rather with the causes, symptoms, and results of psychical disturbance and disease.[38]

To these we now turn.

Chapter 6

MEDICAL THEORIES AND PRACTICES

Popular Images and Medical Concepts

Present-day images of the mad and their treatment in previous centuries are frequently stereotypical generalizations. On the one hand there is the gloomy picture of friendless lunatics, exposed to squalor, punishment and neglect. On the other there is the vision of the mad as endowed with supernatural capacities. Both images may contain a grain of truth. Augustan society for example tended to envisage, and frequently treated, the mad as bestial and subhuman, and the abominable conditions under which a James Norris was incarcerated for years in Bethlem Hospital were not examples of the humanitarianism said to have characterized the Georgian age. Similarly, although the fabulous 'ship of fools' may owe its existence to poetic licence, the 'idiot colony' at Gheel was certainly no chimera.

Neither the gloomy nor the sublime image accurately reflects the heterogeneity of social responses towards the 'abnormal'. Furthermore, these stereotypical representations tend to project the false idea of simple uni-linear development. The history of the mad is construed as a development either from 'better' to 'worse', 'noble' to 'abominable' on the one hand, or from 'scandalous' to 'enlightened', 'dark' to 'light' on the other. The Victorian reformers' picture of Georgian attitudes, for example, reflects the conviction that the eighteenth century's dungeons had been replaced by clean and airy establishments and that the insane had been liberated from abuse, cruelty and neglect. In a similar vein, government officials and medical officers in British India seemed convinced that they had brought with them a superior understanding of mental illness conceiving of madness as a disease susceptible to institutional treatment by medical experts trained in European medicine.

It was also widely believed by the Victorian public in Britain and India that progress had been made in the scientific understanding of insanity. Indeed, the developments in specialized institutional design, legal provision and public concern had been considerable. However, the apparent progress owed much to the nineteenth-century reformers' favourable evaluation of their own activities in relation to those of their predecessors. Their propaganda has been quite durable, so that 'we still tend to view eighteenth-century psychiatry through lenses polished by nineteenth-century psychiatric reformers', taking the contemporary characterization of early nineteenth-century reformed asylum practice too literally.[1] Concepts of insanity in the first part of the century were independent neither of social-political campaigns nor of practitioners' pragmatic considerations. They did not qualitatively transcend late eighteenth-century images and were neither derived from nor constituted a single homogeneous body of knowledge.[2]

If we reject both the stereotypical images of barbaric pre-Victorian conceptions of the mad and the romantic glorification of earlier periods' approach to the irrational, what then *did* characterize Georgian and Victorian notions of mental illness? And to what extent were concepts of madness among the British in India conditioned by ideas in the colonial motherland?

During the Georgian period it came to be recognized that the mentally deranged were not a species apart or creatures without human qualities, but rather that madness was the mental manifestation of a bodily disequilibrium that could in principle affect anybody. Madness was not intrinsic to a particular individual. Nor was it to be explained in religious terms. It arose from a false connection of ideas. Mad people 'err, as Men do, that argue right from wrong Principles' was the slogan coined by Locke.[3] This concept of madness as essentially *human* self-expression accorded with other predominant ideas in Enlightenment Britain. Benevolence and humanitarianism were much admired virtues and the attitude towards groups such as children, women, slaves, 'savages' and in general 'the Other' softened somewhat.[4] This socially committed atmosphere inspired and nurtured ideas of social reform such as Robert Owen's 'new moral world'. It also stimulated that special branch of Scottish common-sense philosophy and social intervention that came into play fully in the early nineteenth century. Philosophically and ideologically the mad had become the target of social concern, paternalism and pity rather than objects of ridicule, persecution or, indeed, veneration.

Yet, the gulf between a permissive philosophical attitude and do-gooder ideology on the one hand and the practical treatment of the mentally ill by their fellow Georgians on the other was often considerable. Official reports on the abuse of the insane in some asylums and workhouses made this clear. Although the Victorians made a point of such revelations as demonstrating their predecessors' unenlightened and inhumane attitudes and practices, their own often failed to meet the philosophers' words and the reformers' ambitions. Things were no different in British India.

The main lesson is that wholesale generalizations about ideas and practices concerning the mentally ill in late eighteenth- and early nineteenth-century British India and Britain are misleading. Practice did not always follow on philosophy's heel. This was partly due to Georgian and (to a lesser extent) early Victorian individualism. Diversity of opinion was the order of the day – in British India as much as in Britain. Recourse was had not only to Locke's epistemology but also to Hobbes' and Pinel's writings as well as to those of Esquirol. Various traditional concepts of Western medical thinking were integrated into these philosophical frameworks: the Hippocratic understanding of human life and disease in terms of body fluids or humours; the conceptual framework of reflexes and neurological circles that developed out of the Cartesian tradition; Newtonian mechanistic models of nerve-fibre-behaviour interactions. The exercise of religious influence, too, was frequently perceived as an important curative aid. Logically incompatible categories were thus used eclectically by practitioners. Terminology was neither precise nor rigorously applied. Furthermore, until the middle of the nineteenth century, doctors in India were not required to specialize in the treatment of the mad, so that many a doctor's basic knowledge of mental illness was often no better than that of any informed layperson. To attempt postulate anything like an 'authoritative definition' of *the* contemporary concept of insanity would be doomed to failure.

Nevertheless, those who dealt with the mentally ill (in Britain and British India) shared some basic conceptual assumptions and their diagnostic and treatment patterns had some distinct features in common. Most doctors were influenced by a Lockean notion of insanity: that madpersons are essentially rational beings who reason rationally, but from false premises; that as all human beings affected by experience, they are not only fallible and prey to illusion but also amenable to re-education and moral guidance; that whilst the *insane* could be cured by manipulating their minds and treating their bodily afflictions, people who were described as *'idiots'* lacked reason and were therefore not amenable to treatment.

Other underpinnings of asylum management in British India included the regime of 'moral treatment' by the Quaker Tukes, who ran the famous York Retreat, and the principle of 'non-restraint', implemented by Hill and Conolly during the 1830s and 1840s in English asylums. The language of 'moral therapy' and 'non-restraint' certainly assumed centre-stage in official reports and regulations. However, these avant-garde and basically non-medical ideas constituted a professional challenge for the medically trained. The Tukes' understanding and treatment of the insane reflected their Quakerism and Samuel Tuke's *Description of the Retreat* conveyed a humanitarian moral rather than any scientific medical analysis. Though usually devoid of any special religious background, asylum superintendents in India were still expected by the Company's authorities and the European public to share the Tukes' approach and to implement what was considered to be the most enlightened available treatment method. Medical practitioners were at pains to integrate a humanitarian perspective (that relied heavily on moral guidance and education) with their medical approach (which was in earlier decades mainly based on blood-letting and later on pharmaceutical intervention). Not surprisingly, the result was a medley of often contradictory treatment methods and a tendency to pay lip-service only to 'moral therapy' and 'non-restraint'.

Medical laypersons such as the Tukes were not the only source for medical officers' official rhetoric. British physicians' medically oriented concepts of madness were being taken up, too, although these would be less frequently referred to in official proceedings than the more accessible vocabulary of 'moral management'. John Brown's notion that virtually all diseases were due to an excess or deficiency of 'irritability' had been influential in Britain from the late eighteenth century and also made its impact on European medicine in India in the early decades of the nineteenth century. The medical board of Bengal stated in a report of 1818 that madness was 'in nearly all its forms' a 'disease of great excitement, and high vascular action'.[5] Dr W. Campbell of Bombay even formulated the 'manifold objects' of his treatment method in reference to Dr Brown's ideas: patients should be supplied with occupations 'incompatible with unhealthy mental excitement'; their 'conditions of bodily health and comfort' should be secured; and 'the amount of restriction, as well as restraint' be diminished; whilst 'confidence, and protection and liberty' had to be increased; and 'painful impressions' be substituted by 'agreeable' ones. In short: the lunatic had to be brought 'into contact' with all that was 'pleasurable and pure and good', while being shielded from exciting and irritating influences.[6] It is largely this Brunonian influence and its central idea that 'great excitement' could best be diminished by depletive techniques (such as bloodletting, emetics, cathartics), to which many asylum inmates during the early decades of the nineteenth century owed their debilitating treatment and in later years assuagement of 'nervous irritability and restlessness' by means of narcotics.

Other reputed English physicians' ideas on madness were well received in British India. William Battie, who 'pioneered clinical psychiatric teaching' at St Luke's in London, had developed a relatively simple classification that combined both moral and somatic aspects.[7] Guided by his practical experience, Battie had come to differentiate incurable 'original madness' (congenital madness, idiocy, brain defects) from 'consequential madness' (the consequence of either physical or mental causes, characterized by deluded imagination, and therefore curable). Seemingly clear-cut classifications like these were highly popular among Indian medical officers. In practice, however, they posed occasional problems, as admitted by the superintendent of the Bombay asylum as late as 1854. On attempting to argue an apparently recovered patient's case for immediate suspension from duty and transfer back home, he pointed out that it was at times difficult to 'draw a distinction between the higher classes of Imbeciles, and those who are nearly sane'.[8] Similarly, the decision whether an inmate was a 'maniac' or an 'idiot' was not always uncontroversial. A patient could suffer from 'mania' or 'melancholia' in the eyes of one practitioner and be labelled a 'perfect Idiot' by another.

Frequent attempts had been made to differentiate 'lunatics' or 'madpersons' (potentially violent or at best unpredictable) from mere 'idiots' and 'imbeciles' (considered harmless and manageable). Medical practitioners encouraged such differentiation as it enabled them to segregate patients and focus scarce institutional funds and staff on the potentially dangerous or suicidal inmates. The intellectually disabled were thought to 'stand in need of more care than the needy, the aged, and infirm, the deformed and the diseased, who tho' feeble it may be in body, have yet sense and intelligence enough to minister to their wants'. But they could do with 'less constant and watchful supervision than the excited maniac or the desponding melancholic'.[9] Some officials such as governor Falkland of Bombay deployed the distinction between 'alleged' lunatics (namely the 'imbecile' and 'idiots') and those who suffered from 'attacks of violence' and 'melancholia' to strengthen their argument for separate and less expensive institutions for the increasing number of the socially harmless Indian and Eurasian asylum inmates.

The categories of 'idiocy' and 'insanity' were difficult to separate – not only for the European public but also for many a medical officer lacking expertise in the treatment of the mentally ill and intellectually disabled. Of census officials in the 1870s, for example, it was reported that the 'distinction between insane persons and idiots has not been understood by the enumerators', so that 'inmates of lunatic asylums have in many cases been returned under the latter title'.[10] Asylum superintendents, too, frequently used the terms 'idiot', 'maniac' and 'madman' interchangeably or as vaguely descriptive of certain behaviour patterns rather than as delimited concepts.

Apart from conceptual and terminological ambiguities, systems such as Battie's were very workable. Despite an apparent psychological emphasis, they could easily accommodate somatic concepts: the mind was clearly located in the brain, with blood vessels and environmental and 'moral' factors exerting some influence. Consequently external stimuli such as blisters, leeches, douches and cooling tonics as well as regulated diet and alcohol, purgatives and emetics, exercise and recreation would contribute towards cure. Further, concepts such as Pinel's 'partial insanity' and Prichard's 'moral insanity' could be used alongside the basic idiocy-madness delineation. Like the understanding that both 'moral' and 'intellectual' forms of insanity could be complicated by epilepsy and general paralysis, such systems were seldom strictly applied in practice.

'Moral' Therapy, 'Mental' Illness and 'Physical' Derangement

It is well established that most early nineteenth-century classifications were ultimately based on a somatic notion of mental illness – even when terms such as 'moral insanity' were used. The language of 'moral' therapy and management and the understanding that madness could be caused by either 'physical' or 'moral' factors has tended to mislead today's historians and psychiatrists who sometimes simply equate 'moral' with what is nowadays understood by 'psychological'. Further, the talk of 'moral therapy' and 'moral causes' of insanity had a ring of ethical judgement about it. For example, lack of moderation was seen to cause certain forms of madness and the 'superintendent's Moral Power over the Patients' was considered to be one of the central features of the proper management of the mentally ill.[11]

The contemporary practitioner applied these terms in a less definitive way and they gained their meaning from a medical cosmology that differed fundamentally from present-day mainstream psychiatry, psychosomatic medicine and clinical psychology. 'Intemperance' for example could be referred to as either a 'moral' or a 'physical' cause of mental illness. Factors that might today be considered as psychological – the death of relatives, exposure to unknown conditions and anxiety – were then usually considered to be 'moral' in the sense that a particular event, state or condition had a decisive impact on the whole person, affecting the whole system and finally becoming localized in the brain, thereby giving rise to 'a disease called insanity'.[12] Given such basically *somatic* understanding of what came to be known as *mental* illness, the contemporary belief that many forms of insanity were (in theory if not in practice) amenable to cure by medicine just as easily as whooping cough, measles and the like, seemed plausible.

Medical practitioners during the earlier decades of the nineteenth century did not usually elaborate on the exact circumstances of their patients' cases. To them it was a clearly established fact that in India attacks of madness could 'in almost every instance be traced to exposure to the sun, hard living and other irregularities, exciting the action of the heart and blood vessels, and producing unusual determination to the head'.[13] The special circumstances of colonial life, and in particular of the military servant's life in barracks and camps, were considered as unwholesome and characterized by 'peculiar temptations'. Service in the Company's army 'in the plains of India' tended to be seen as 'one unbroken course of physical degradation', bound to exert 'depressing influences on the mind and body'.[14] Factors such as unhygienic conditions as well as widespread abuse of the liquor bottle, sexual activities, loneliness, boredom and 'constant observation of sickness, suffering, and death' were cited as the main reasons for many European regiments' disciplinary problems and their poor state of health.[15]

'Moral' factors seem to have had precedence over 'physical' causes in exciting insanity. And there were numerous references to the importance of practising 'moral' treatment. But asylum doctors frequently attended merely to the physical diseases (such as cholera, dysentery, diarrhoea, fever and syphilis) suffered by patients in addition to or independently of their insanity. In the Calcutta asylum, for example, the madhouse proprietors were supposed to ensure that patients were treated with 'kindness and humanity'.[16] But they faced occasional criticism of the absence of a 'more intimate and more cultivated experience of the varied forms and shades of mental diseases as well as a more enlarged philanthropy than appears to be…available in the Asylum'. The medical officer on duty for routine visitations and emergencies had only limited say in the asylum. And for 27 years 'moral treatment' was reported by the medical board of Bengal to have been 'unaided and uncontrolled by the ordinary medical Attendant', who 'understood his duty mainly to consist in affording his advice and assistance to the bodily ailments of the Insane'. He would see patients only on admission, discharge, or when something went wrong, but would not usually have any impact on their daily life in the institution. The situation was somewhat different in Bombay and Madras where the medical officer was also the administrative superintendent. But even here the medico usually restricted his activities to the more narrowly medical parts of his task and left any day-to-day 'moral management' to his subordinates.

The impression therefore emerges that the concept of 'moral therapy' in British India was much talked about, but rarely seen. During most of the early nineteenth century medical officers did what they had been trained for: they checked inmates' physical conditions, prescribed drugs in cases of acute restlessness, violence and melancholic states, and carried out post-mortem examinations. Their approach was in practice narrowly medical. This became more apparent towards the middle of the century when the bodily basis of insanity and consequently the precedence of medicine over management were championed. During that period, the craze for phrenology and post-mortem investigations as well as British doctors' attempts to defend their expertise against laypersons' and moral therapy enthusiasts' transgression on what they considered to be their own exclusive sphere of expertise reached the colony. W. A. Green, civil surgeon of Dacca, pointed out in 1856 that insanity was 'essentially a physical derangement and alteration of the normal structure of the brain'.[17] He mentioned Indians' 'noisy, and exciting, and exhausting' festivals and national ceremonies as well as 'indulgence in exciting and intoxicating drugs and liquors' as causative factors, alongside others such as 'visceral disease of the thorax and abdomen'. But it was clear that he considered insanity *not* to be 'a mere psychological disease, a merely strictly mental malady independent of physical change of the brain'.

The emphasis had now shifted from vague postulation of blood vessels and brain activity as necessary intermediaries in madness, to the apparently clinically grounded belief that insanity was basically attributable to 'molecular alterations in the fibrous arrangement and tissue of the brain'.[18] During a period of six years, civil surgeon Green had cut open and dissected the skulls of 76 of his deceased asylum patients following a medical approach that he claimed to share with doctors such as Forbes Winslow and J. C. Bucknill in England.

Green was not the only one who took an interest in his dead patients' brains, but his post-mortem findings were never unequivocally confirmed by other practitioners. The superintendent of the European and the 'native' lunatic asylum in Bengal, Dr T. Cantor, too, spent a great deal of time and effort dissecting not only brains but also any other organs. During 1856 and 1857, 13 of his patients had died.[19] According to the asylum records, five of them had suffered from 'diseases of the nervous system' (hemiplegia, abscessus cerebri, apoplexy, exhaustion), another five from 'endemic diseases' (dysentery, diarrhoea, cholera), whilst two had died from 'old age' and one from 'caries'. Cantor was anxious to provide as thorough a scientific analysis as possible. He made use of the microscope, drew up brief medical histories of his post-mortem subjects and left no organ untouched.

Unlike his colleague in Dacca, however, who had found 'morbid conditions of the brain' in all of his numerous corpses and believed that 'insanity consists of, and is essentially a physical derangement and alteration of the normal structure of the brain', Cantor could offer no such unequivocal results.[20] Of those who had suffered diseases of the nervous system only three were 'attended with structural change of the brain'.[21] In the endemic cases only two 'presented cerebral, in addition to the ordinary phenomena', and in the remaining three cases the former 'caries' patient's brain substance had softened and one old inmate's lateral ventricles 'contained a quantity of serous effusion', while the remaining geriatric patient 'exhibited no cerebral morbid appearances'. Cantor had to admit that because of the prevalence of various physical diseases supposedly alongside mental illness, it was difficult to differentiate the psychological impact of the one from the organic consequences of the other.

Apart from the general assumption that madness had in the last instance an organic basis, both Green and Cantor drew more differentiated theoretical conclusions from the wealth of data they so meticulously gathered. In this they were typical of that brand of Victorian doctors who dissected a number of their former patients, collated the resulting data in effusive tables, yet frequently failed to convincingly substantiate their conceptual statements with the concrete evidence. At a period when the collection of artefacts, memorabilia and objects *per se* was widespread, statistics were by force of their factuality and richness of data perceived as scientific in themselves. Unaided by the authors, we are therefore left to rely on our own analytical aspirations if we wish to work out what the numerous tables of post-mortem data might tell us.

Nineteenth-century statistics in general are of questionable usefulness as reliable evidence of medical realities. They do however reveal the professional orientations and assumptions of medical officers. To nineteenth-century practitioners a multitude of raw data was a mark of the methods and rationale of modern science in that sphere of medicine that had hitherto mainly been linked with speculation on the importance of lunar influences or with more practical concerns such as asylum design, 'moral management' and 'non-restraint'.

Green's and Cantor's clinical specialization and their passion for post-mortems were not shared by every asylum doctor. Dr W. Campbell of the Bombay Asylum took greater interest in the stories his patients had to tell about their family life and work experiences. To him asylum inmates' previous history was more useful for diagnostic purposes than the scalpel. Yet, despite some variation in styles of management and medical specialization, images of insanity had in general begun to converge towards the middle of the nineteenth century.

It was however not until the 1860s and 1870s that concepts of mental illness became more narrowly defined and the treatment of the mad more homogeneous. Events such as the Indian revolt of 1857 and the change of guard from 'John Company' to the British Crown in 1858 were instrumental here, as was the British doctors' Bucknill and Tuke publication in 1858 of their eminent *Manual of Psychological Medicine*. Green's and Cantor's clinical emphasis therefore foreshadowed a new medical paradigm in the treatment of the insane emerging towards the second half of the nineteenth century.[22] Narrowly somatic concepts of insanity that tended to view the mentally ill as irrevocably mad were then in vogue. There was no more question that insanity was a 'disease' rather than an 'affliction', as had so frequently been argued during previous decades. Bucknill expressed the belief that when a person was 'lunatic' he was 'lunatic to his finger ends'.[23] It was such ideas that were to quickly find favour with medical officers in India. Awareness of the high incidence of alcoholism, malnutrition and infectious diseases and the continuing accumulation of uncured patients inside institutions constituted a breeding ground for assumptions of hereditary and organic factors and of racial predisposition to mental illness.

European colonial society as a whole had turned more race- and class-conscious, more hostile towards the indigenous population and less permissive towards marginalized social groups. When the spread of Western education had enabled Indians to compete successfully for posts in the Indian Civil Service, the British could (as Ballhatchet pointed out in his work on *Race, Sex and Class under the Raj*) 'no longer assert their right to power on grounds of superior knowledge or intellect: instead they turned to arguments of racial superiority'.[24] Psychological models of 'impaired identity' did not, of course, necessarily lend themselves to the discriminatory treatment of patients of different social and racial groups in lunatic asylums.[25] They were however conducive to a colonial ideology that had begun to legitimize the colonial order of things by postulating certain races' and social classes' inability to gain the noble and indispensable characteristics that allegedly distinguished those men who then ruled British India.

Diagnostics and Therapeutic Practice

Despite the growing political and social importance of hereditary and narrowly medical concepts of madness and mental capacity, classificatory and diagnostic categories did not change to any great extent. The classic delineation of 'mania', 'melancholia' and 'dementia' was still as common in the 1850s as it had been during the 1800s. Dr Cantor, for example, included 'mania', 'dementia', 'idiocy', 'amentia', 'melancholia', 'monomania' and 'moral insanity' in his list of what he called 'forms of disease' (alongside categories less commonly used in asylum nosologies, such as 'phrenitis', 'hemiplegia', 'splentitis' and last but not least 'syphilis consecutiva').[26] This listing, though idiosyncratic and by no means exhaustive, contained the most distinct diagnostic categories then used in England and British India.

Other practitioners' classifications differed mainly in the extent to which they used subdivisions of the central disease categories. Dr Campbell not only differentiated 'dementia' from 'congenital idiotcy' [sic] but also split it up into two distinct entities: 'imbecility' and 'fatuity'.[27] The remaining categories he restricted to 'mania', 'melancholia' and 'monomania'. However much Cantor's and Campbell's schemes may be seen to differ in classificatory emphasis, they both still referred to a modified version of the same classical Greek system. Yet, the extent to which physical diseases (such as phthisis, epilepsy, scurvy, syphilis) and insanity were assumed to be connected, varied. Dr Arbuckle, one of Campbell's predecessors in Bombay, for example, integrated into his nosological scheme conditions such as 'epilepsia', 'puerperal' and geriatric problems and 'general paralysis'.[28] He however saw certain diseases as not so much inextricably linked with some forms of insanity, as manifest in addition to them. Arbuckle therefore used the descriptive categories of 'epilepsia and imbecility', 'epilepsia and mania', 'senile fatuity', 'general paralysis and idiocy' and 'puerperal mania'. Campbell in contrast classified the majority of patients as suffering from 'idiocy', 'imbecility', 'mania', 'melancholia' and 'chronic insanity'. In comparison with Arbuckle, then, Campbell's nosology differs slightly in conceptual outlook in that the latter concentrated on patients' mental affliction. Nevertheless, both perceived and treated the various physical diseases as mere 'complications' of insanity.

From today's point of view these kinds of classifications may well appear to have been based on quite diverse terms if not different concepts. They would not conform to criteria such as those now laid down in the various versions of the *Diagnostic and Statistical Manual of Mental Disorders* (DSM) developed and marketed by the American Psychiatric Association, and the *Manual of the International Statistical Classification of Diseases, Injuries, and Causes of Death* (ICD) produced by the World Health Organization. Modern mainstream psychologists and psychiatrists who have been reared on the principle that any therapeutic measure ought to be based on sound diagnostics might doubt the extent to which the treatment applied in the various asylums in nineteenth-century British India could have been efficacious. Contemporary practitioners were, in contrast, but little prey to the illusion that only allegedly clear-cut and sophisticated diagnostic labels could, if not guarantee, then at least be a requisite for the cure or improvement of a patient's condition.

Men like Cantor used categories such as 'mania' and 'dementia' as descriptive rather than generic terms. 'Mania' basically was how a person behaved and appeared to another. It was the term used to describe the symptoms rather than the disease itself: the disease a patient suffered from was 'insanity', the way it manifested itself was through 'mania' or other 'forms of the disease'. Consequently, a patient might have been categorized as a 'maniac' at one time and as 'imbecile' or suffering from 'moral insanity' at another. Not only would the diagnostic label vary with the patient's symptoms, but the treatment, too, would follow suit. Treatment was inherently geared towards what some of today's psychologists aspire to: a person-centred and flexible approach in diagnostics and therapy rather than a procedure that centres on psychological testing and screening. Unsatisfactory as symptom-based assessment and therapy may now be judged to be, it constituted in some instances an advantage to the patients. Inmates were, after all, responded to on the basis of the symptoms from which they were suffering at any one time, rather than only in accordance with an earlier diagnosis. Such an approach could at its best facilitate the establishment of an immediate and spontaneous therapeutic rapport and understanding between inmate and doctor. Some patients did in fact perceive treatment that aimed at symptom relief as beneficial – even when they did not stand much chance of permanent cure. They were grateful for the doctor's attention to their mental problems and physical ailments, and appreciated attempts to improve their well-being.

However, one has to caution against too enthusiastic an interpretation of what might seem to be an understanding and well-meaning person-centred therapy. On the basis of the little knowledge doctors had been able to accumulate on the aetiology of madness, they were not usually in a position to ameliorate the condition of those patients who suffered from mental problems brought on by infections, malnutrition, neurological diseases, or the like. The diagnosis 'mania', for example, could have been applied to capture the observable behavioural features that are associated with such different conditions as chorea (a neurological disease), syphilis, typhoid, malaria, 'reactive psychosis' (for example 'battle shock'), or even 'feigned madness' (in pursuit of furlough or discharge). Similarly, people can become paralyzed or demented due to a multitude of very different factors, some of which require very specific medical or psychological intervention in order for treatment to be persistently effective. Hardly ever would the progress of conditions, such as paralysis, for example, be halted. Generally, therapeutic measures were applied on a basis of trial and error and whilst in some cases this method proved most successful, it could be fatal, or at least ineffective, in others.

Aetiology and Prognosis

Contemporary practitioners made some effort to discover their patients' history to determine the cause of their mental problems. The causes usually listed in case records ranged from more specific ones, such as 'fear to be caught by a tiger', 'drunkenness', 'hereditary', 'fall' or 'sudden fright', to vaguer terms such as 'vice' or 'exposure to unknown conditions and influence of tropical climate'.[29] However, apart from increasing a practitioner's knowledge and perhaps his understanding of a patient's personal circumstances, awareness of preceding events had little influence on either diagnosis or treatment.

Prognosis would also be but marginally influenced by aetiological considerations. There were some exceptions. The 'weak-minded' or 'idiots' were expected to be beyond cure, although improvement was occasionally reported. General paralysis of the insane also warranted little hope, although the connection of this with syphilis had not yet been recognized. The causal link of *Delirium Tremens* to alcohol abuse had been established, but reliable prognostications were hard to come by. In general, doctors possessed some inkling about who among their patients would be likely to remain under medical care for prolonged or intermittent periods. This knowledge stemmed more from longstanding practical medical experience and the continued observation of an individual patient's state of mind than from recognition of any specific feature in a patient's previous history.

The connection between suspected causes, diagnosis, therapy and prognosis was anything but clear. Why then would doctors bother to discover patients' personal and medical history? First, from early in the century, such investigation was required by regulations echoing those of the metropolitan commissioners in lunacy in London. This was driven by the Company's desire to curtail public expenditure by tracing any solvent relatives. By the middle of the century, many asylum superintendents attended to the mad but aspired also to some explanation of their proteges' mental problems. The nature of insanity was still surrounded by 'mystery' and speculation about its origin was rife among medicos and the laity. By the 1850s asylum doctors found themselves having to provide medical reasons for unreasonable behaviour to maintain their public and self-image as experts.

Most doctors in British India thought that medical practice in the East had unique features and that certain physical and mental conditions tended to differ in appearance and intensity (if not in nature) from those experienced in more temperate climes. More thorough statistical documentation and analysis were considered to be a necessary step towards exploiting Company medicos' special 'position' in the East and 'its true value to science'.[30] This ambition to enhance knowledge of the aetiology of mental illness among Company servants was not universally shared. In many instances only lip-service was paid to the hospital boards' demand that a summary statement of the supposed causes should be provided alongside more detailed information on each patient's previous history. Failure to provide such data cannot always be blamed on medicos' indifference or their lack of conviction that insight into the causes would be practically relevant. The wealth of detail available to superintendents by the regimental doctors, when they transferred patients from military stations to European asylums, varied considerably. It was, more often than not, decidedly sparse. Superintendents, on admission of new patients, had often to rely on hearsay from the attendants and invalid soldiers looking after the patients en route.

Even when information on patients' pre-history was available, it was not always easy to determine what may have caused mental breakdown. For example, Seaman Charles C. was admitted to the Calcutta asylum shortly after the Indian revolt of 1857/8.[31] He had been suffering from syphilis and 'intermitting fever'. A history of alcohol abuse was suspected. He had also gone through the traumatic experience of service up-country during the 'Mutiny', leaving him in constant, and perhaps well-grounded, fear that he was 'going to be killed'. In this by no means rare case, the combination of diverse organic and psychological factors made any attempt to determine *the* cause of the patient's mental condition inappropriate.

There are many cases where several factors preceded patient's mental problems. Doctors typically focused on one or two of them. Several decades before C., in 1820, a gentleman by the name of W. P. had been under treatment in the Madras lunatic asylum for exactly two decades.[32] P., who had led a 'chequered life', was formerly a surgeon, then a captain in the Nizam of Hyderabad's service, and had also acted as 'a Player at the Theatre of Madras'. He had been received into the madhouse in 1800 because of his 'extreme eccentricity of behaviour'. He remained there until removed to England 20 years later. In the transfer papers P.'s doctor mentioned that the patient had contracted syphilis a few years prior to admission to the Madras asylum. Nevertheless, the doctor attributed the 'Mental Malady' to more general 'disappointments followed by habits of intemperance'. It obviously was tempting for P.'s doctor in 1800 to point to one single suspected cause rather than a complex interaction of a variety of factors. Today's diagnosticians, too, would no doubt like to isolate a single cause such as the possibility of a syphilitic origin, and a valid diagnosis of *lues zerebrospinalis* might occasion a partially efficacious treatment. But P.'s doctor did not possess the pharmacological means to do so, even had he determined syphilis to have been the presumed cause. The one thing the doctor was sure about was that 'there is not the smallest hope of this patient's recovery'.[33] P. indeed remained an in-patient of Pembroke House, London for nearly 30 more years, before dying of old age.

Treatment

If aetiological considerations had at best a minor impact on the therapeutic process and prognosis, of what then did treatment consist? And what was the rationale behind it? There is of course no straightforward answer to this question. Medical practice differed from practitioner to practitioner and changed over the course of the nineteenth century. In the earlier decades the use of mercury concoctions was widespread, as was the bleeding of patients. These remedies were increasingly regarded as non-effective and even detrimental in a climate such as that of British India. This was particularly so for insane Europeans. Purgatives and tonics, emetics and douches became the main favoured remedies.

P.'s fellow inmates in the Madras asylum of 1820, for example, seldom received any other treatment than purgatives, leeches and blisters. As often as not no treatment was applied. It was considered enough to make patients take exercise and to occasionally restrain them by means of the strait-waistcoat, or to administer cold douches. Of P. it was said by his doctor that 'Medicine is rarely required', because 'exercise is freely taken' so that the patient's 'alvine evacuations' were regular. Restraint was imposed on him merely during the 'periods of the New and full Moon when he is apt to be noisy and abusive'.[34]

By the middle of the century, doctors tended to supply more detailed information on what appears to have been a somewhat more diverse and versatile approach towards medical treatment. Take again the case of Charles C. On admission to the general hospital C. was still suffering from an 'intermitting fever' contracted during his service up-country.[35] He was also 'low spirited' and had an ulcer on the penis. C. had arrived in hospital 'weak and anaemic' and remained so despite active treatment aimed at stimulating the body and counteracting physical weakness. He was put on a supportive regime of 'quinine and other tonic medicines', nitrate of silver lotion applied to the ulcer and a nourishing diet 'of half mutton, with half a pound of extra bread and a pint of beer'. When necessary, 'occasional aperients' were prescribed in order to counteract any visceral sluggishness.

C.'s treatment seemed appropriate not only for his poor physical state, but also for his steadily deteriorating mental condition. He was 'always in very melancholy mood', so that pharmaceutical measures that thwarted the 'nervous exhaustion' seen to be characteristic of melancholia were particularly indicated.[36] However, the medical regime did not lead to the expected improvement. The hospital surgeons consequently entertained doubts as to whether the general hospital was the proper place for the patient. C. presented with 'delusions', hearing people 'continually talking about him' and being firmly convinced that 'he shall never be allowed to go out of the gate'. Initially his doctors had assumed that these symptoms were merely a result of the fever. Only a few nights after his arrival he had already been 'delirious and troublesome'. His mental condition then was duly assessed as being 'periodic depending on the fever'. But C. soon had 'delusions also between the paroxysms'. It was obviously difficult for the two doctors involved to make sense of these mental symptoms, which were, apparently, unrelated either to the 'fever' or to the alleged syphilitic affliction. They had seen many patients suffering from alcohol-related problems and on recognizing some symptoms with which they were familiar, they speculated as to whether C. had not had a history of intemperance. Yet, they were unable to 'find out that he ever was a hard drinker'.

C.'s eventual transfer to the Calcutta madhouse in February 1860 seemed appropriate at the time. A madman in the hospital wards was irritating for other patients and tended to stretch the hospital surgeons' expertise. It also posed practical problems, as it was difficult to keep such patients securely locked up. On one occasion, C. tried to squeeze himself through the window in his cell. He might have succeeded had he not got stuck in a gap between the venetians and been found hanging in there 'as far as the waist'.[37] In the asylum C. would not be able to even get half-way out of the window. This institution was built to detain more and less willing patients inside its walls. Unlike the general hospital, the asylum specialized in various means of restraint. Furthermore, the medical regime in the asylum under surgeon T. Cantor was specially geared towards restraint and sedation of patients. Dr Cantor favoured a highly regulated regime and regarded discipline, order and strict surveillance of patients as crucial pillars of modern asylum management. He also emphasized the importance of medical experts taking charge and considered medical prescriptions the centre-piece of treatment. In place of tonics C. was made to take hyoscyamus, a drug that, depending on dosage, could be used as a narcotic or sedative.[38]

Medical treatment in the hospital certainly differed from that in the asylum. This discrepancy could however not simply be blamed on hospital surgeons' lack of experience with insane patients. On the contrary, their specific remedies and overall medical approach were well grounded in contemporary medical and emergent psychiatric theory. The feature that differentiated the two approaches most is the extent to which an attempt was made to not merely control patients' mental conditions by means of medical prescriptions, but to pharmacologically subdue them, and to discipline their behaviour to make them fit in with an ordered and regulated institutional life. The medical subjugation of patients is particularly prominent in Dr Cantor's approach to C. and his sedative regime. It is striking because C. had been described as 'quiet, but desponding, of few words and of melancholy expression of countenance'.[39] The patient therefore constituted at most a minor threat to discipline, unlike those inmates suffering from, say, maniacal excitement.

Admittedly, C.'s tendency to take to his heels for 'fear of being murdered' would have been annoying and unacceptable for asylum staff. Further, his treatment also included some tonic and rejuvenating measures such as 'exercise in the open air', cold baths, 'light reading' and 'light generous diet'.[40] But, it remains the case that even a harmless and withdrawn patient such as C. could be sedated. Unlike the strait-waistcoat, which was used when need arose, Cantor's routine recourse to sedation pre-empted the patient's attempts at escape but also prevented him from experiencing the external world other than through a drug-induced haze. Asylum staff may well have found it easier to control the patient; any benefit to C. himself is less clear. He continued to be haunted by frightful images.

The 'pharmacological straitjacket' was routinely used by Cantor as a preventative instrument for institutional discipline. The pharmacological approach, i.e. the use of sedatives and narcotics, became increasingly prominent in the management of growing asylum populations in the second half of the nineteenth century. Cantor's regime prefigured this tendency.

C.'s case highlights the controlling aspect of medical treatment. But Dr Cantor's preference for sedation was not typical of *all* early nineteenth-century medical practice in India's lunatic asylums. Nor was the application of tonic medicines for the physically debilitated and mentally depressed representative of the treatment in general hospitals. Other medical officers in India may well have administered stimulant remedies or applied blisters to C.'s head in order to substitute a real for an imaginary pain. Or they may have taken to various different approaches in succession on a trial-and-error basis. Treatment patterns varied widely, not only from institution to institution but also with each medical officer.

The Question of 'Non-Restraint'

There were certain areas of asylum management, however, in which convergent adaptations were made to circumstances seen to be peculiar to a colonial situation. The question of what forms of restraint to use vexed all asylum superintendents in British India. By the 1840s in Britain the doctrine of 'moral therapy' and 'non-restraint' had become imperative for those asylum doctors who considered themselves as advanced and humanitarian. Doctors in British India were consequently under pressure from the Company authorities and the parliamentary board of control who expected them to implement the most 'enlightened' regimes of the times.

Yet, conditions in asylums for Europeans and 'natives' in India were (like those in many average institutions in Britain) not particularly conducive to what had by the middle of the century culminated in the demand for the 'total abolition of restraint'.[41] Insane patients, in particular the Europeans, frequently presented extremely violent behaviour, with unexpected attacks on attendants and fellow inmates, and sometimes almost continuous rages. Towards the end of the century such 'maniacs' would usually be doped with narcotics. Earlier, attempts were made to weaken their vital energies by repeated use of purgatives and emetics. However, a debilitating regime could not be sustained for prolonged periods. Before the widespread use of the pharmacological strait-waistcoat, medical officers were therefore often at a loss as to how to pacify patients who constituted a threat to themselves, to others and, last but not least, to asylum discipline.

For 'non-restraint' enthusiasts there was but one alternative: 'classification – watchfulness – vigilant and unceasing attendance by day and by night – kindness, occupation, and attention to health, cleanliness, and comfort, and the total absence of every description of other occupation of the attendants'.[42] Dr Cantor echoed this view when he proclaimed that 'kindness is the real substitute for mechanical restraint'.[43] In addition to 'gentleness and watchfulness', attendants should be endowed with 'a certain tact, which, by abstaining from unnecessary interference, knows how to avoid aggravating excitement'. It was however exactly in regard to their staff's incapacity to adequately display such a characteristic that medical officers in India floundered. First, the low salary paid to European attendants was unlikely to attract employees amenable to the aims and ideals of 'moral therapy' and 'non-restraint'. Then, there were few positions available for Europeans, as Company officials were eager to cut down on staffing costs. The asylum in Bombay employed in 1852 only one European to look after up to 15 European patients. Cantor had in 1857 only two – an apothecary and an overseer – on his books.

For ordinary day-to-day management scarcity of European attendants was offset by a greater number of Indian servants. In Bombay 16 Indians were permanent staff, in addition to one ward attendant for every three European inmates (in contrast to one for every seven 'Natives'). However, Indian staff were considered unsuitable for dealing with violent European inmates. There were several reasons for this. Medicos were convinced of the 'utter want of moral and physical courage of the native attendants'.[44] They also doubted whether an Indian could ever be expected to display that 'tact' that was necessary if they wanted to 'protect and control Insanes' without having recourse to mechanical restraint.

With insufficient European keepers, an alleged absence of integrity of character in Indians and a notorious 'lack of means of proper seclusion and of padded rooms', superintendents admitted that 'mechanical restraint could not with safety entirely be dispensed with'.[45] This view had been held from the early decades of the nineteenth century onwards. Although it was then couched in softer terms, the means used (coercion-chair, restraint-couch, manacles, and fetters) appeared harsher. By the 1850s the situation was reversed: the argument against 'total non-restraint' had become more insistent and previously used instruments of restraint were 'consigned to the lumber-room'.

Although superintendents like Dr Cantor conceded that 'the system of non-restraint, in the ordinary acceptance of the term was established as the rule of the Asylum', straitjackets and thick fingerless leather gloves were still used 'in cases of extreme violence' and whenever 'the malady intrinsically disqualifies Insanes'.[46] Examples of the latter case were instances in which patients were subject to 'secret vices'. In the more 'pernicious' forms of this 'indelicate malady' (which was also known as 'masturbational insanity') even straightforward remedies such as 'seton dorsi penis, vesicantia to the palms of the hands, and internal remedies' were according to Cantor known to fail and, what is more, such 'vices' were 'capable of eluding the strictest vigilance'. It was here that 'a pair of rigid fingerless gloves, joined together' and applied at bedtime had proved 'the only effectual remedy'.

The possibility of completely doing away with mechanical restraint had, however cautiously expressed, always been questioned. Even in Britain the discussion focused on what sort of restraint was least unacceptable rather than on 'total abolition'. During the 1850s, however, a further dimension was added to the whole topic. Dr Cantor, for example, made it very clear that mechanical means were only second-best and only to be used 'till internal remedies allow the mechanical adjuncts to be discontinued'.[47] The pharmaceutical approach was to take precedence under usual circumstances. Only when medication failed, as in such exceptional cases as when 'during paroxysms of fury after the failure of soothing treatment, tonsure of the head, or application of vesicantia cannot be safely effected', was the temporary application of a strait-waistcoat, for example, considered legitimate.

Cantor summarized his advocacy of pharmaceutical and mechanical restraint with an argument that might in its essentials even be used by present-day practitioners objecting to critics' enthusiastic suggestions of reforms. In daily humdrum asylum practice medical officers were frequently, he argued, confronted with specific problems such as whether to apply fracture splints in order to 'protect some insanes against their propensity of inflicting sores on certain parts of the body'.[48] He concluded derisively that these kinds of mundane problem 'those philanthropists who have carried the non-restraint system to its greatest perfection, have left subjects of speculation'.

The one argument that was considered most compelling in the advocacy of mechanical restraint was that of patients' resistance to coercion by man-handling. Doctors Laycock and Noble, cited by Cantor as well-known practitioners in Europe, held mechanical appliances 'preferable to a struggle between Patient and Attendant'.[49] The observation of several of Cantor's predecessors in the three European asylums in India also indicated that 'mechanical appliances cause[d] less excitement than physical force'. Cantor adapted this point to Indian conditions when he talked of a 'peculiar condition well deserving of notice' and characteristic of the treatment in India of European lunatics, namely 'the sense of humiliation or degradation which certain classes, Soldiers and Sailors in particular, are in the habit of attaching to coercion by the hands of native Attendants'. He recalled instances 'in which convalescents who distinctly remembered the paroxysm, have expressed gratification at having escaped the "shame of being laid hands upon by natives" '.

This was strong language, but one that befitted a topic that touched upon the disturbing possibility of physical encounters between Europeans and Indians. After all, Cantor produced his reflections on 'non-restraint' in May 1858, when the Indian revolt or 'Mutiny' was not yet completely quelled. What then shocked the European community at large was akin to what upset the superintendent's and his patients' minds: the nagging idea and obnoxious reality that Europeans were being vanquished by native colonials.

In the event Cantor provided what he called a 'remarkable illustration' of Europeans' and in particular of military servants' dread of being 'laid hands upon by natives'.[50] A field officer, 'distinguished no less by his services than by his gentlemanly qualities' had gone mad while on leave in another colony. He had been locked up in a jail and subjected to bodily restraint. On arrival in the Calcutta asylum 'his expression was wild, and he was inclined to become violent'. Cantor asked the obvious question: 'Should he not be locked up and coerced by natives?'. A clear answer followed: 'Certainly not', since this officer was a European and a gentleman. Thus, of course his 'word not to escape was sufficient'. The patient recovered following a 'successful course of treatment', revealing during Cantor's first subsequent visit that the 'appeal to his honor...had effectually subdued him'. Moreover, it was the 'freedom from mechanical restraint, and of all things, from being coerced by natives' that had made 'a deep impression upon him'.

The gentleman slumbering in this patient had obviously conquered the madman's maniacal inclinations. In the case of this officer the suspicion that early nineteenth-century 'moral therapists' and 'non-restraint' advocates succeeded in replacing external coercion by internal restraint, manacles and physical force by psychological pressure, is certainly confirmed. The patient's inclination to stick to his word may have been motivated as much by the ambition to live up to the expectations of a gentleman as by the unsettling thought of having to undergo the humiliation of physical restraint by 'native' colonial subjects. Yet, the aim and result were the same: the patient was not to be coerced by Indians. It was for the representatives of British rule to mete out blows, and not for its vassals.

Social Discrimination, Racial Prejudice and Medical Concepts

Racial prejudice was omnipresent in British India – inside institutions and in the community at large. So were considerations of social precedence. This was expressed in a system of classification of inmates that required segregation according to social class. The language used to describe European gentlemen's and gentlewomen's mental condition was less harsh and seldom even vaguely derogatory as it was so often in the case of lower-class soldiers and pauper patients. The gentlemanly yet violent officer under Dr Cantor's care was referred to merely as a man whose 'intellect had been affected', just like the gentleman 50 years before him, who had suffered loss of fortune and reason simultaneously, had been considered to have been affected by temporary 'weakness'. Lower-class patients, in contrast, tended to be talked of as 'perfect Idiots' and 'maniacs'. Diagnostic categories such as 'mania' or 'dementia' were of course also applied to first-class patients. But they would rarely be mentioned in case reports and official correspondence other than euphemistically. Some practitioners, like surgeon J. Callagan of the Madras medical board, went so far as to disapprove of 'dooming' gentlemen 'to the humiliating scenes of a madhouse' where they would have 'nothing before them but the distracting gestures and clamours of Maniacs of all Countries and of the lowest Ranks in life'.[51]

Social discrimination was not confined to the expatriate community. It was characteristic also of Indian society. Nor was it altogether unheard of among Georgians and Victorians in the colonial motherland. Widespread as discrimination may have been among the various peoples in Europe and India, examples of British snobbery certainly highlight the extent to which racial and social exclusiveness influenced medical perceptions impinging even on areas of such marginal socio-political importance as lunacy provision. Ubiquitous social discrimination and its colonial pendant, racial prejudice, were highly instrumental in the formation of judgements on the comparative incidence and the nature of mental illness among the various social classes and races. In fact, apart from the question of restraint, racial and social sentiments were more prominent in no other area of asylum medicine than in the epidemiological discussions of the 1850s. Views on the spread of mental illness in British India were of course influenced by conceptual developments in Europe. In Britain Dr J. Reid expressed in 1808 the commonly held view that 'Madness strides like a Collossus in the country'.[52] One explanation was that the perceived steady increase in the incidence of insanity could largely be accounted for by the progress of civilization. The more people were exposed to modern ideas and ways of life, and the more educated they became, the more susceptible would they be to mental derangement. People who lived in remote and secluded areas (such as the Welsh mountains and the Scottish highlands, or in the allegedly less developed parts of southern Europe), were considered to be not only simple and contented but also psychologically more stable. Susceptibility to mental derangement was the price a nation had to pay for its spiritual and economic progress.

Matters were, however, more complex in British India. During the earlier decades British doctors here too tried to convince themselves that madness was less widespread among simple village folk and unsophisticated Indian town dwellers. By the middle of the nineteenth century, they had to employ considerable mental acrobatics to uphold this argument. Assumptions of inherent racial inferiority had become particularly pronounced in India when Western education was being propagated by liberal reformers as the 'panacea for the regeneration of India'.[53] Once that Indian, but English-educated, middle class, a 'class of persons Indian in colour and blood, but English in tastes, in opinions, in morals, and in intellect' had been raised and had begun to compete with the British for positions in trade and administration, the liberal vision of India's regeneration had turned sour. Consequently the view gained prominence that by virtue of education alone an Indian could never be civilized enough to become a legitimate candidate for government positions (or, for that matter, for insanity!).

By the time of the 'Mutiny' at the latest it was widely believed that an Indian could intrinsically never rise above what was considered to be the inferior characteristics of his race. Was it not a fact that Indians were naturally endowed with inferior mental capacity? Was not their mind possessed of a 'feeble texture' that could easily become unhinged? Such considerations were, of course, rather at odds with the view that 'uncivilized' people were less prone to mental problems, especially as it was simultaneously held by many Britons that Indian culture possessed some strangely irritating aspects. Indian festivals and national ceremonies were almost always described as noisy, exciting and exhausting, and therefore of a kind to 'frequently upset the mind'.[54] It was also believed that Indians were prone to 'indulgence in exciting and intoxicating drugs and liquors'. Such alleged cultural idiosyncrasies would typically be interpreted by British expatriates as a 'rife cause of insanity in the feeble minds of the poorer Asiatics'.

Such cross-currents of racial and cultural preconceptions engendered conflicting and contradictory claims on the spread and incidence of insanity in British India. Civil surgeon W. A. Green of Dacca argued within a few lines of the very same volume of the *Indian Annals of Medical Science* in 1857 that the 'occurrence of insanity amongst the natives of India and the East is probably as frequent, if not more so, than in the temperate and colder climates of other parts of the world', and that the 'mind of the Bengallee and Hindoostanee is not assailable in so many points as that of the lower orders of European countries'.[55] The hackneyed contemporary argument was that the European lower classes' tendency to succumb to vice and liquor was due to a lack of willpower. Green, operating from a racial perspective, argued that compared with Indians, lower-class Europeans' 'intelligence and range and grasp of apprehension (and consequent obnoxousness [sic] to so many more stimulating and deranging influences)' were 'so much greater'. To complicate the argument even more, Green went on to point out that 'the very poorer order in other countries' were 'numerically less insane than the same class in the East'. He attributed this particular phenomenon to the alleged fact that 'the feeble texture of the mind of the later class' would 'more readily' give way 'before the disturbing causes'. Still he claimed that these cases were 'fewer far than those by which the minds of a more generally enlightened people are liable to be disconcerted'.

However muddled Green's analysis, it contained the main strains of thought then widely held by medical experts and laity. In a more blunt fashion these had been consolidated to the position that however much

> natives of this country suffer in comparison to Europeans as regards their intellectual endowments and perceptions, they are so far gainers in being considerably less disposed to become the subjects of disease implicating that delicate and highly-organized structure, the brain and its appendages, the functions and physiology of which are so little understood, but which are seen to be more or less susceptible of derangement as we advance or descend in the scene of civilization.[56]

Another, more differentiated but still racially biased, view was that of Calcutta-based surgeon J. Macpherson, published in the *Calcutta Review* in 1856. He held that insanity was not more prevalent in civilized countries, it simply assumed a different form and was taken more notice of than among the 'ignorant', 'uneducated' and 'superstitious' of countries such as India.[57] He also criticized other 'popular views' on this topic such as those of Copland, Prichard and Oesterlen in Europe. Macpherson shared their belief that 'southern nations are less subject to insanity than northern ones', but denied that 'Europeans going to the Tropics are especially liable to attacks of the nervous system'. He labelled accounts of Europeans' physical and mental debilitation in the East as reminiscent of the 'fabled "Armida's Garden" of Ariosto' and dismissed them as pictures 'too highly colored' and drawn 'only from the accounts of travellers'.

Although Macpherson's arguments went against some of the central planks of contemporary mainstream medical thought, his report on 'Insanity among Europeans in Bengal' was frequently referred to by colleagues. He was one of few asylum superintendents who had attempted to prove their general point statistically. However, Macpherson himself admitted to having significantly underestimated the incidence of madness. Regimental returns like those published in 1855 on the 1st Bombay European Regiment showed that 'affections of the mind form a large item' in the statistics on invalids, namely 14 per cent.[58]

East is East, and West is Best

Reflections such as those of Macpherson and, to a lesser extent, Green were part of the more general debate on whether Europeans could ever become acclimatized to conditions in the East. This debate was a harbinger of medical ideas about degenerationism, so influential during the second half of the nineteenth century. It was also of great socio-political importance, as signalled by an article by assistant surgeon A. S. Thomson, published in the *Transactions of the Medical and Physical Society, Bombay* in 1843: 'Could the Natives of a temperate climate colonize and increase in a tropical country and vice versa?'[59] The question of whether white settlers should be allowed in British India had always been controversial. In favour of white colonization was the argument that 'our Indian possessions' would be rendered 'more secure'. But this view was undermined by the lingering danger of settlers 'throwing off' the yoke of the mother country' (as with the Spanish and Portuguese in South America and the American War of Independence).[60]

In the realm of medicine the question was also controversial. The central concern here was whether European settlers could 'live and produce pure offspring in India'.[61] It was feared that they were 'likely to become degenerate' within a few generations – 'from the climate and connexion with low ignorant women'. The evidence was open to diverse interpretation though. People of Dutch and Portuguese descent were considered 'both mentally and physically degenerate'. This was said to be a good illustration of 'the injurious effect of climate on the descendants of Europeans in India'. It was however conceded that 'their constitutions are rendered more adapted to the climate by a union with the aboriginal inhabitants'.[62] Nevertheless, was it not the unequivocal experience of many a British mother that her children frequently suffered debilitating illnesses and did not thrive easily in India's plains? Was it not with difficulty that European children were 'brought to maturity' and that soldiers in European regiments were kept alive and good-humoured without the privilege of sick-leave to England, which was such a vital factor in the preservation of the health of higher-class civil servants and officers? 'There is little doubt', concluded Dr Thomson of the 14th Light Dragoons, 'the tropical parts of the world are not suited by nature for the settlement of the natives of the temperate zone' and if the children of the British were not sent back to Europe they would become 'stunted in growth and debilitated in mind'.[63]

The theory of 'acclimatization' prominent among doctors in Britain concluded that even the British could eventually habituate themselves to the alien Indian climate. But most expatriates tended to agree with Thomson that the Indian climate was inhospitable and dangerous. It burnt the skins and got on the nerves of those reared under the gentle drizzle of maritime conditions. The enduring 'solar myth' emerged of the power of 'heat and dust' to set off a whole range of unpleasant ailments, from prickly heat to insubordination, from heat-stroke to adultery and manslaughter, depression and paralysis, nervous exhaustion, irritability and neurasthenia. Victorians tried to control many aspects of life in the East and took measures to ameliorate its detrimental effects. Civilians' office hours implied an early rise and a long break at midday; the military started its troop marches and physical training before sunrise; and only mad-dogs and few Englishmen were found outside without their specially designed solar 'topees'.

Yet, it was not just the Indian climate in its narrowly meteorological sense that upset Europeans. It was the whole range of social and cultural trappings peculiar to their life in the East. The majority of British expatriates had with every decade of the nineteenth century become increasingly hostile towards their Indian environment. This apparently abounded in hidden dangers, hosted uncivilized and barbaric (yet intriguing and fascinating) practices and had a dire effect on the unwary European. One expression of this is the insistence by most medical officers on European lunatics' early repatriation. Medicos held that although 'it affords good ground...for a recommendation that [a patient] should not return to duty', it 'must be admitted, that in no instance, after an attack of insanity should a man be permitted to remain in circumstances and relations which are obviously so likely to lead to a relapse'.[64] Even the apparently cool, salubrious hills relatively isolated from the madding Indian crowd of the plains were no substitute for the green and pleasant lands of home.

Providing European lunatics with a passage to England owed its instant appeal to the European community's endeavour to permanently dispose of embarrassing members of the white ruling class as much as to medical considerations of the healing power of repatriation. Furthermore, the deportation policy fitted in with the contemporary mainstream image of the nature of British colonialism in India. The British hold of its 'Indian possessions' was usually taken to be a lasting engagement, culminating during the heyday of the British Raj in an 'illusion of permanence'. But there also existed strong doubts as to the extent to which a place like India could ever become permanent home to the British. The majority of British expatriates considered themselves basically as transients who took up the highly lauded burden of the white man and would eventually, in health or sickness, sanity or madness, be shipped back to 'Blighty'. There was no better cure for an ailing and alien Company servant than 'home'. This view, cherished by most Europeans in British India, was shared by the majority of the medical profession, becoming the centre-piece of the treatment of the European insane.

Medical authorities in British India drew heavily on the concepts and treatment methods prevalent in the colonial motherland. But these principles were refracted through the distorting prism of the colony's severe climatic conditions and its peculiar racial and social ideology. A special, colonial brand of medical theory and practice emerged: British in origin, but adapted to the requirements and morals of a local community of expatriates.

Chapter 7

CONCLUSION: 'MAD DOGS AND ENGLISHMEN ...'

In tropical climes there are certain times of day
When all the citizens retire, to tear their clothes off and perspire.
It's one of those rules that the biggest fools obey,
Because the sun is much too sultry and one must avoid
   its ultry-violet ray —
Papalaka-papalaka-papalaka-boo. (Repeat)
Digariga-digariga-digariga-doo. (Repeat)
The natives grieve when the white men leave their huts,
Because they're obviously, absolutely nuts —

                              Noel Coward

In the preface to his famous *Folie et Déraison* Michel Foucault suggests:

> To write a history of madness would mean to produce a structural study of
> the historical whole – notions, institutions, legal and police measures,
> scientific concepts – that imprison a madness that can never be restituted to
> its natural state.'[1]

No such total analysis in the structuralist sense has been attempted here.
Nevertheless, the aim has been to reconstruct the history of madness among
those treated by the British during 'John Company's' time as completely as
surviving sources allow. The treatment of the European and Indian mentally ill
in British institutions has been analyzed in relation to colonial ideology, state
policy and legislation; the important role of public opinion 'at home' and in the
colony in the construction of treatment methods and administrative control
measures has been highlighted; and the reconcilability of commercial interests,
colonial ideology and humanitarian motives has been discussed.

Further, the comparatively early and successful intervention by the colonial
state in the 'lunacy sector' has been related to the persistent endeavour of
Company officials and of the expatriate community more generally to preserve

the image of the European elite as formidable and impeccable colonial rulers. Institutional arrangements in the three main asylums were determined by the same colonial ideology – notwithstanding local specificities and contingencies. The institutions reflected the values and practical concerns of colonial society at large: the *idée fixe* of social precedence and concomitant snobbery; the extension of class barriers into racial prejudice and distance; and an insistence on racial and social segregation that during the nineteenth century increasingly widened the gulf between the British ruling elite, its lower-class compatriots and the Eurasian and Indian communities – inside as much as outside the madhouse.

The policy of sending the European insane back to Britain was a particularly poignant reminder that the Company acted swiftly to make 'invisible' those who might otherwise have tarnished the image and self-perception of the British as a mentally and physically superior people. Despite relative numerical insignificance, the institutionalization and repatriation of the European mentally ill retained a symbolical importance that went far beyond its proximate function of controlling socially harmful and embarrassing individuals and 'subjugating unreason'.

Furthermore, the madhouse became one of the markers of socio-economic and scientific progress and of the 'superior' qualities of Western civilization. Towards the middle of the nineteenth century the rising social status of medical practitioners and their professional recognition helped to advance the case for Western medicine. Although it was conceded that 'the study of Insanity' was a 'branch of medical education utterly ignored by the licensing bodies' and that there were 'few in the public service who can be supposed to know anything about it', medical doctors became promulgators of the enduring colonial myth of Western medicine as an excuse if not legitimation for colonial rule.[2]

For those made 'invisible' by institutionalization and deportation, and at the receiving end of medical and psychological intervention, confinement was not always unwelcome. Patients belonging to all classes of society as often as not preferred treatment in the institutions to the harsh life in military barracks and civil stations. Despite gradually deteriorating provision and increasing discrimination against lower-class inmates, the lunatic asylums in British India turned only slowly from refuges or temporary receptacles to 'total institutions'.

Medical paradigms and treatments varied considerably. They were derived largely from the imperial motherland. Restricted and vague as they were in scope, they evolved in harmony with the specific environmental, ideological and social demands of the wider colonial context: the tropical climate necessitated less drastic medication and a modification of architectural principles; tribute was paid to racial superiority and social snobbery by substituting the doctrine of 'total non-restraint' with the advocacy of occasional mechanical restraint; medical reasons were repeatedly advanced against the view that Indians could ever be raised above their 'inferior' mental and physical 'nature'; and the assumption was rejected that Europeans could gradually 'acclimatize' themselves to life in the tropics without becoming mentally and physically degenerate themselves.

Many questions on 'European madness in colonialism' still remain unanswered. For example, did people with different regional origins, temperament and historical and religious backgrounds experience life in the Company's army and navy in distinctly different ways? It seems unlikely that a mixed bag of English, Welsh, Scots and Irish as well as recruits from various European countries would always respond to the call of duty in a uniform way. There is much evidence in patients' case reports that communication problems between national groups and quarrels about religion and national idiosyncracies were implicated in soldiers' and sailors' psychological breakdown as commonly as was the maliciousness and brutality of some non-commissioned officers and the disregard for recruits' self-esteem and personal integrity so characteristic of the military.

Yet, because of the multitude of factors that typically over-determine the development of mental problems, it is difficult to single out 'regional origin' as a distinctive discrete cause of emotional breakdown or madness. Nevertheless, the prevalence of nationalism and of feelings of 'regional identity' seems to be an important factor in Company employees' history of mental illness. This uncomfortable speculation is contrary to one of the enduring myths of empire, of an unshakeable 'esprit de corps' amongst individuals charged with colonial rule. A deeper analysis of patients' life stories and of institutional histories would be required to substantiate these speculations.

A further query is whether the 'social control' aspect of emerging psychiatry was in fact not much weaker than commonly suggested. If it is true that somatic disease, malnutrition and alcoholism accounted for the majority of deaths and hospital admissions; that hospitalization in the asylum on account of mental illness was a comparatively rare occurrence; and that emotional breakdown and mental problems were, in the military, dealt with first of all by punishment or temporary furloughs, whilst civilians fell within the purview of the police, then the case for 'social control' may indeed appear negligible. In turn this raises doubt about the suggestion of increased 'medicalization' or the process by which ever more personal ailments and areas of social life become subject to medical attention and control during the early nineteenth century.

The notions of 'social control' and 'medicalization' are easily overdone. A phenomenon as complex as that of madness in colonial rule cannot easily be explained by a few catch-words. There was more to it than the 'control of the rabble' and the advance of medicine, or the 'subjugation of unreason' by the discourses of reason and science. The most relevant of these factors have been touched upon. We may legitimately conclude that the confinement of the mentally ill and, more so, European medicine (and emergent psychiatry) were eminently instrumental in the maintenance and legitimation of the colonial endeavour. The crucial point is not what institutionalization, repatriation and the work of European medicos actually achieved on a *practical* level. Performance in this respect was as a matter of fact quite restricted during most of the nineteenth century. The central point is not of medicine as an effective 'tool of empire', but of the persistent *myth* of medicine as a tool of and excuse for colonialism. It is here, at the point where medicine was, and still is, considered as a cogent reason for colonization that we need to reconsider social control, the all-embracing nature of medicine and the tools of empire.

Finally, not much has been said about the impact on Westerners of India as a culture. Can we not reasonably assume that the variety of cultural heritages of India would have left a strong impression (not to say occasional confusion) on Europeans' minds? Was it not the case that the British conceived of themselves as strangers in an alien place? What about any perceived 'Indianness' of the ailments that affected Europeans in India? Exposure to unfamiliar cultures is after all nowadays conceived of as a psychological stressor and as a possible factor in the development of behavioural and mental problems. The possibility of 'culture shock' appears the more legitimate since contemporaries occasionally warned that life in the tropics could leave its mark on Europeans' physical and mental health.

There are several reasons why this question is difficult to answer. First of all, nineteenth-century medical practitioners and scholars *did* attest a crucial role to the Indian environment. But the way in which India's 'alien sky' was seen to impact on Westerners differed fundamentally from today's conception. We would today talk of an alien environment in terms of 'culture', 'customs' and 'beliefs'. Contemporaries tended to elaborate on the 'climate' (heat and cold, atmospheric pressure, marsh effluvia), on the quality of the water and on geographical features. Early nineteenth-century medical thought was still indebted to the Hippocratic corpus of *Airs, Waters, Places* and the prevalence in far-away places of environmental conditions so different from those of the British Isles did much to revive this classical body of thought. Further, the process of colonial penetration widened the scope for environmental theories by enabling Westerners to come into contact with peoples of hitherto scarcely known lands. This fuelled speculation on how the various living habitats had formed their 'character' and might influence the well-being of European traders, soldiers and civil servants raised under more temperate conditions.

The first half of the nineteenth century was of course the period of 'moral management', 'moral insanity' and the understanding that 'moral' as well as 'physical' factors could lead to madness. Yet, this connection between morals and insanity did not refute the environmental paradigm. Both Hippocratic theory and moral managers conceived of madness ultimately within a somatic framework. Although the talk of 'moral management' and 'moral causes' was widespread, the theory did not impact practice to the extent it had in some model institutions in Britain. Ill-health in the tropics was by and large linked to exposure to the sun, high humidity and the emanations from the earth. Even the age-old connection between lunar constellation and nervous irritability found new esteem.

It is to a large extent this notion of well-being in terms of bodily functions and environmental and moral influences that makes it difficult for a modern observer to determine whether 'culture' as we conceive of it today was seen as – or was in reality – a relevant factor in the causation of mental derangement. This problem is further exacerbated by the fact that preventative and curative medicine relied heavily on physical intervention and manipulation. Environmental influences were quantifiable and therefore open to ascertainable standards: a carefully measured amount of food and drink, of space or air per person in barracks, hospitals and asylums; a clearly circumscribed set of times for daily outdoor exercise and regular shower baths and ablutions; restricted contact with the outside world; and routine transfer to the air and place of long-term patients' native land. These were the important determinants (though not guarantees) of a healthy institutional life in the tropics. Not surprisingly, then, 'culture' appears even in the more elaborate of case reports on asylum patients as a mere (unquantifiable and therefore irrelevant) background factor and at best as part of an unhealthy basic environment.

The possibility of 'cultural alienation' as a factor in Europeans' mental derangement is further obscured by the fact that the British tried to *avoid* contact with local culture during the Victorian period. Extending the barrier of social class characteristic of late Georgian and Victorian Britain, the ruling elite in India kept itself aloof from Indians and imposed restrictions on the extent to which its lower-class compatriots could interact with the indigenous population. 'Going native' became increasingly disapproved of over the decades. It was seen permissible only for a few eccentrics or irrecoverably 'Indianized' Brits of otherwise impeccable social standing. One example was Sir Charles Metcalfe, a distinguished Company official, whose political achievements and local knowledge were appreciated, although his extensive Indian family was rarely publicly referred to.

The ordinary soldier and sailor had little occasion to socialize with Indians on equal terms and was spared estrangement by unfamiliar sights and customs. Marriage quotas were restricted and although in the nineteenth century the number of Indian camp-followers was considerable, with porters, water-carriers, horse-grooms, bacon-*wallahs*, prostitutes and the like, they were out of bounds during most of the day. Segregation was less easily enforced at sea ports where hawkers, beggars, harlots and hands hired by the hour would hover around East

Indiamen moored in the harbour. Yet, here, too, the 'native' parts of towns were no-go areas. The contact that did occur between men of the West and people of the East was largely that between Indians who offered their services and Europeans who made use of them. This was bound to create that combination of racial and sexual dominance, assumed superiority and petty-oppression (rather than induce feelings of cultural alienation) that is typical of interpersonal relationships in colonial situations.

Nineteenth-century British colonialism is particularly renowned for its transplantation of class barriers and its distaste for social intercourse with its colonial subjects. It is perhaps not surprising then that the majority of Europeans would rarely have a chance to go 'doolally' from encounters with Indian 'culture'. Although the authorities warned that observation of Indian rituals and ceremonies might unhinge the mind of Indians and Europeans alike and 'often revealed anxiety at the thought of British soldiers wandering beyond the controlled environment of the cantonment into mysterious places where they might be infected with dangerous diseases and tempted into Oriental vices',[3] it was the climatic conditions of India or an 'exposure to unknown conditions' that were suspected by asylum superintendents as causes of madness.

A further dimension is added to the question of cultural causation by the high incidence of disease, malnutrition, alcoholism and death on account of cholera, fevers, liver problems, diarrhoea and dysentery. Any speculation about single-factor causation of insanity therefore appears ill-conceived. It may well be that people were likely to die from some physical disease before they even had a chance to develop any adequate mental symptoms.

Finally, it should not be forgotten that most Europeans in British India were in the military or navy. Within these institutions mental and emotional problems became conspicuous primarily on account of their behavioural consequences. Although madness was considered to be a disease amenable to treatment by medical experts, any deviation from the norm of disciplined behaviour was interpreted as insubordination and routinely dealt with by disciplinary means. Military authorities were concerned primarily with correction of the undesirable behaviour rather than the alleviation of personal suffering. There was little sympathy for consideration of subordinates' personal difficulties in coping with the demands of military life. The language of 'disgraceful and highly irregular conduct and neglect of duty to the prejudice of good order and discipline' was heard in barracks and mess decks, not talk of emotional breakdown, nostalgia, or cultural alienation. Even in those few cases in which transfer to the lunatic asylum occurred, medical certificates echoed the discourse of discipline. The reputed 'burden' the white man had to bear in the East was to a large extent that of his own culture: the burden of restrictive British institutions, of parochial social communities and of the malice and vindictiveness of superiors and comrades.

It remains somewhat misleading to graft today's interest in 'culture' onto nineteenth-century socio-political realities and medical cosmologies. The more so as what really is at stake is the economic, social and psychological impact of colonial rule. The concern with 'culture shock' and 'cultural alienation' is then more likely to distract from the far more pertinent topic of colonial penetration. Modern theories on cultural influences by and large conceive of different cultures as independent realities and rarely take into account that it is the relationship between social groups that conditions the scope and limits of contact between their cultures. In regard to colonial history this means the relation of rulers to the ruled. Balandier emphasized this point when he asserted that it was myopic to investigate the contact between 'cultures' in isolation from the contact between racial groups, disregarding the socio-political reality of colonial groups.[4] One of the main aims of this study has been to locate 'madness' in its wider socio-political context and to elucidate further the profound effect colonialism had not only on Indians but also on the dominant and subordinate groups of the European community. In that sense the intention has been to provide a critical account of 'madness in colonialism' that goes beyond both Balandier's partisanship for a politically inclined scientific analysis and the popular image of the Raj as a place where only 'Mad dogs and Englishmen go out in the mid-day sun'.

PRIMARY SOURCES

Official Correspondence, British Library, London, Oriental and India Office Collections

Dispatches from London

Civil Judicial Despatches to Bengal (Lower Provinces)
Commercial Despatches to Bengal
Financial Despatches to India
Judicial Despatches to Bengal
Legislative Despatches to Madras
Legislative Despatches to India
Military Despatches to Bengal
Military Despatches to Bombay
Military Despatches to India
Military Despatches to Madras
Political Despatches to India
Public Despatches to Bengal
Public Despatches to Bombay
Public Despatches to India
Public Despatches to Madras
Public Works Despatches to India

Letters (dispatches) to London

Judicial Letters received from Madras
Legislative Letters received from India
Military Letters received from Bengal
Military Letters received from Bombay
Military Letters received from India
Military Letters received from Madras
Public Letters received from Bengal
Public Letters received from Bombay
Public Letters received from India
Public Letters received from Madras

Government Proceedings / Consultations

Bengal (Lower Provinces) Civil Judicial Proceedings
Madras Judicial Proceedings
Madras Legislative Proceedings
India Legislative Proceedings
Proceedings of the Legislative Council of India
Bengal Military Proceedings
Bombay Military Proceedings
India Military Proceedings
Madras Military Proceedings
Bengal Public Proceedings
Bombay Public Proceedings
India Public Proceedings
Madras Public Proceedings
Bombay Public Works Proceedings

India Office Files / Selected Material

Board's Collections
Court's Minutes
Miscellaneous Letters, received
Miscellaneous Judicial Letters, received and sent
The Records of Pembroke House and Ealing Lunatic Asylum, 1818–1892
Revenue, Judicial, and Legislative References

Private Papers / Demi-Official Correspondence

Oriental and India Office Collections: MSS

Richard Compton
John Luck
A Grenadier's Diary

Centre of South Asian Studies, Cambridge

Mrs Montgomery's Letters

Official Publications, Governmental Reports / Commissions

The British Library, London

Report from the Select Committee on the state of criminal and pauper lunatics and the laws relating thereto, 1807
Reports from the Select Committee on the better regulation of madhouses in England, July 1815, April–June 1816
Reports of the Metropolitan Commissioners in Lunacy

Hansard's Parliamentary Debates
Parliamentary Papers, House of Commons
Parliamentary Papers, House of Lords
Census of the Island of Bombay (Bombay: Education Society Press, 1864)
Memorandum on the Census of British India of 1871–72 (London: Eyre and Spottiswoode, 1875)

Wellcome Institute for the History of Medicine Library

London Royal Commission on the Sanitary State of the Army in India, 2 vols. (London: Eyre and
    Spottiswoode for HMSO 1863)

NOTES

Preface

1 J. McCulloch, *Colonial Psychiatry and 'The African Mind'* (Cambridge: University Press 1995).
2 See for a fuller assessment of recent historiographic trends: W. Ernst, "Beyond East and West. From the History of Colonial Medicine to a Social History of Medicine(s) in South Asia", *Social History of Medicine* 20, no. 3 (2007): 505–24.
3 F. Fanon, *Black Skin, White Masks* (London: Pluto 1986 [1952]), p. 74.
4 A. Nandy, *The Intimate Enemy* (Delhi: Oxford University Press 1974).
5 G. Spivak, "Subaltern Studies: Deconstructing Historiography (1985)", in D. Landry and G. MacLean (eds), *The Spivak Reader* (London and New York: Routledge 1996), 203–35, p. 214.
6 H. Bhabha (ed.), *Nation and Narration* (London: Routledge 1990). H. Bhabha, *The Location of Culture* (London: Routledge 1994). G. Spivak, "Can the Subaltern Speak?", in C. N. and L. Grossberg (eds), *Marxism and the Interpretation of Culture* (Urbana: University of Illinois Press 1988), 271–313. S. Amin and D. Chakrabarty (eds), *Subaltern Studies 9: Writings on South Asian History and Society* (Oxford: University Press 1996). D. Chakrabarty, *Provincializing Europe: Postcolonial Thought and Historical Difference* (Princeton: University Press 2000).
7 For 1980s and 1990s appraisals of Foucault's work in English, see O. Faure, "The Social History of Health in France: A Survey of Recent Developments", *Social History of Medicine* 3, no. 3 (1990): 437–53. H. C. E. Midelfort, "Madness and Civilization in Early Modern Europe: A reappraisal of Michel Foucault", in B. C. Malament (ed.) *After the Reformation: Essays in Honor of J. H. Hexter* (Philadelphia: University of Pennsylvania Press 1980), 247–65. C. Jones and R. Porter (eds), *Reassessing Foucault: Power, Medicine and the Body* (London: Routledge 1994).
8 The principle of 'less eligibility' aimed at deterring people from claiming poor relief. Conditions in workhouses were to be worse than those outside.
9 P. Gray, *The Irish Famine* (London: Thames and Hudson 1995).
10 T. M. Devine, *Clanship to Crofters' War: The Social Transformation of the Scottish Highlands* (Manchester: University Press 1994). E. Richards, *The Highland Clearances* (Edinburgh: Birlinn Books 2000).
11 E. Hobsbawm and G. Rude, *Captain Swing: A Social History of the Great English Agricultural Uprising of 1830* (New York: W. W. Norton and Company 1973).
12 F. A. Bruton (ed.), *Three Accounts of Peterloo by Eye-Witnesses* (Manchester: University Press 1921). J. Marlow, *The Peterloo Massacre* (London: Papp and Whiting 1969).
13 V. G. Kiernan, *Lords of Human Kind: European Attitudes Towards the Outside World in the Imperial Age* (Harmondsworth: Penguin 1972), p. 33.
14 D. Arnold (ed.), *Imperial Medicine and Indigenous Societies* (Manchester: University Press 1988).

Chapter 1: Introduction: Colonizing the Mind

1 E. Stokes, *The English Utilitarians and India* (Delhi: Oxford University Press 1982 [1959]), p. XI.

2 E. Eden, *Up the Country* (London and Dublin: Curzon 1978 [1866]), p. 70.

3 S. C. Ghosh, *The Social Condition of the British Community in Bengal, 1757–1800* (Leiden: Brill 1970), p. 73.

4 C. Allen, *Plain Tales from the Raj. Images of British India in the Twentieth Century* (London: Macdonald Futura 1981 [1975]), p. 19.

5 Maud Diver, 1909, quoted in Allen, *Plain Tales*, p. 57.

6 P. Spear, *The Nabobs. A Study of the Social Life of the English in eighteenth century India* (London and Dublin: Curzon 1980 (1932, 1963)), p. 126.

7 C. A. Moore, 1953, quoted in V. Skultans, *English Madness. Ideas on Insanity, 1580–1890* (London: Routledge & Kegan Paul 1979), p. 33.

8 Eden, *Up the Country*, p. 77; Horace Walpole, quoted in Skultans, *English Madness*, p. 27.

9 Moore, writing on Abbé le Blanc, quoted in Skultans, *English Madness*, p. 33.

10 P. Woodruff, *The Men Who Ruled India* (London: Jonathan Cape 1971 [1953]), vol. I, p. 380.

11 Spear, *The Nabobs*, p. 148.

12 F. Fanon, *Peau noire, masques blancs* (Paris: Editions du Seuil 1952). F. Kramer, *Verkehrte Welten. Zur imaginären Ethnographie des 19. Jahrhunderts* (Frankfurt am Main: Syndikat 1977). M. Leiris, *Die eigene und die fremde Kultur* (Frankfurt am Main: Syndikat 1979). P. Rack, *Race, Culture, and Mental Disorder* (London and New York: Tavistock 1982).

13 See for example Woodruff, *Men Who Ruled India*, p. 180.

14 See for examples notes by E. Thompson, in Eden, *Up the Country*, pp. 397–8.

15 Woodruff, *Men Who Ruled India*, p. 180.

16 'My Dear Mother ... if for ever o a due, sell not my ole close'. Gunner John Luck's letters from India, 1839–1844 (London: India Office Library and Records, manuscripts), introduction.

17 Eden, *Up the Country*.

18 *Letters from Richard Compton*, 1856–1858 (London: India Office Library and Records, manuscripts), 22-6-1857.

19 Md Mil Proc, 23-3-1821.

20 T. Williamson, *The East-India Vade-Mecum* (London: Black, Parry & Kingsbury 1810), vol. 2, p. 320.

21 M. Foucault, *Folie et Déraison. Histoire de la folie à l'âge classique* (Paris: Librairie Plon 1961), p. VII. (Le 'morose etat civil de[s] prisons').

22 Ghosh, *Social Condition*, p. 1.

23 Spear, *Nabobs*, p. 6.

24 Ghosh, *Social Condition*, p. 99; Spear, *Nabobs*, p. 10.

25 Ghosh, *Social Condition*, p. 74.

26 Spear, *Nabobs*, p. 22.

27 I. Munro, quoted in Ghosh, *Social Condition*, p. 70.

28 Ghosh, *Social Condition*, pp. 65, 70.

29 Spear, *Nabobs*, p. 26.

30 V. G. Kiernan, *The Lords of Human Kind. European Attitudes to the Outside World in the Imperial Age* (Harmondsworth: Penguin 1972 [1969]), p. 37.

31 Spear, *Nabobs*, p. 137.

32 Spear, *Nabobs*, p. 140.

33 E. J. Hobsbawm, *Industry and Empire. From 1750 to the Present Day* (Harmondsworth: Penguin 1981 [1968]), p. 88.

34 Resident at Indore to I Govt, 31–10–1838.

35 Spear, *Nabobs*, p. 140.

36 Anon. *Observations on India*, 1853, quoted in Spear, *Nabobs*, p. 141.

37 Charles Grant, quoted in A. T. Embree, *Charles Grant and British Rule in India* (London: Allen and Unwin 1962), p. 169.

38 *Royal Commission on the Sanitary State of the Army in India* (London: Eyre and Spottiswoode for HMSO 1863), p. XXIV.

39 Spear, *Nabobs*, p. 63.

40 Ghosh, *Social Conditions*, p. 89.

41 Stokes, *Utilitarians*, pp. XII, XIII.

Chapter 2: Madness and the Politics of Colonial Rule

1   P. Spear, *The Nabobs. A Study of the Social Life of the English in eighteenth century India* (London and Dublin: Curzon, 1980 [1932, 1963]), p. 70.

2   Bm Minute, 7–9–1850.

3   Separate Minute, Bombay, 7–12–1850.

4   P. Spear, *The Oxford History of Modern India, 1740–1975* (Delhi: Oxford University Press 1984 [1965]), p. 65. Spear, *Nabobs*, p. 79.

5   P. Woodruff, *The Men Who Ruled India* (London: Jonathan Cape 1971 [1953]), vol. I, p. 153.

6   Mill, quoted in E. Stokes, *The English Utilitarians and India* (Delhi: Oxford University Press 1982 [1959]), p. 48.

7   Mill, quoted in Stokes, *English Utilitarians*, p. 48f.

8   Stokes, *English Utilitarians*, p. 51.

9   Carlyle, quoted in Stokes, *English Utilitarians*, p. 50.

10 Bm Minute, 13–7–1820. Bm Med B to Govt, 3–7–1820. Bm Med B to Govt, 3–8–1820.

11 Bm Med B to Govt, 3–7–1820. Bm Med B to Govt, 19–6–1820.

12 Bm Med B to Govt, 3–7–1820. Bm Med B to Govt, 19–6–1820. G. O. Bombay, 4–9–1827. Quarter Master Cen to C-i-C, Bombay, 8–8–1826. Bm Asylum Report, 31–3–1852.

13 Bm Med B to Govt, 24–8–1850. Bm Pub L, 16–4–1851. Suptd Surgeon Karachi to Commissioner in Scinde, 1–2–1850. Bm Minute, 22–3–1850. Commissioner in Scinde to Govt, 12–9–1850. Bm Minute, 14–10–1850. Govt Bm to Govt India, 29–11–1853.

14 Bm Med B to Govt, 22–6–1852.

15 India Pub D, 9–11–1853.

16 A. T. Embree, *Charles Grant and British Rule in India* (London: Allen and Unwin 1962), p. 169.

17 Chief Mag Calcutta Police to Govt, 30–1–1840.

18 Bg Pub L, 21–7–1818.

19 Spear, *Oxford History*, p. 210.

20 D. MacDonald, *Surgeons Twoe and a Barber. Being Some Account of the Life and Work of the Indian Medical Service (1600–1947)* (London: Heinemann 1950), pp. 108, 134. Minute by Lord Dalhousie, 14–6–1852.

21 Resolution, Md Govt, 13–12–1808.

22 Bm Med B to Govt, 18–3–1801.

23 Bg Hosp B to Govt, 4–2–1788.
24 Stokes, *English Utilitarians*, p. 34.
25 V. Skultans, *English Madness. Ideas on Insanity, 1580–1890* (London: Routledge & Kegan Paul 1979), p. 111.
26 Skultans, *English Madness*, p. 112.
27 Skultans, *English Madness*, p. 109.
28 W. Ernst 'The Establishment of "Native Lunatic Asylums" in early nineteenth-century British India', in G. J. Meulenbeld and D. Wujastyk (eds) *Studies on Indian Medical History* (Groningen: Egbert Forsten 1987).
29 Beardsmore to Bg Med B, 2–5–1836. A. Halliday, *A General View of the Present State of Lunatics, and Lunatic Asylums, in Great Britain and Ireland, and in some other Kingdoms* (London: Underwood 1827), p. 65.
30 Bg Pub D, 5–2–1851.
31 Bg Med B to Govt, 21–2–1818.
32 Bg Govt to Med B, 17–3–1818.
33 Bg Med B to Govt, 10–3–1851. Historical evidence of abuse can be read either as evidence of the relative inadequacy of the system (as suggested here), or as evidence that the system worked quite well in that it did indeed discover and act upon such abuses. Additional evidence which shows that nothing effective was done about revealed problems, and that the same problems recurred in the same institutions, is needed to discriminate between these two possible hypotheses. See for such evidence: Ernst 'Establishment of "Native Lunatic Asylums".
34 Bg Mil D, 26–8–1818.
35 Stokes, *English Utilitarians*, p. 10.
36 Spear, *Nabobs*, p. 55.
37 Bg Mil D, 8–4–1816.
38 Stokes, *English Utilitarians*, p. 60.
39 Stokes, *English Utilitarians*, p. 35. Stokes, *English Utilitarians*, p. 46.
40 Stokes, *English Utilitarians*, p. 35.
41 Grant, quoted in Stokes, *English Utilitarians*, p. 34.
42 India Pub D, 17–4–1857.
43 *Royal Commission on the Sanitary State of the Army in India* (London: Eyre and Spottiswoode for HMSO 1863), p. XVII.
44 *Royal Commission*, p. XIX. Mortality (all causes, 1814–1833) soldiers: 69 in 1,000; officers: 38 in 1,000.
45 Bg Med B to Govt, 26–8–1835.
46 India Pub D, 18–9–1839.
47 Chief Mag Calcutta Police to Govt, 30–1–1840.
48 India Pub D, 1–12–1852.
49 Bg Comm D, 13–3–1833.
50 Md Citizens to Govt, 28–11–1851.
51 W. Ernst, 'Madness and Colonial Spaces. British India, 1800–1947', in Leslie Topp, James Moran and Jonathan Andrews (eds), *Madness, Architecture and the Built Environment* (London and New York: Routledge 2007).
52 Minute by Govr Falkland, Bombay, 7–9–1850.
53 Note by Sec to Bg Govt, 9–6–1852.
54 'Out of sight and out of mind. Insanity in early nineteenth-century British India', in J. Melling and B. Forsythe (eds), *Insanity, Institutions and Society* (London and New York: Routledge 1999), 245–67.

55 G. A. Berwick, MD to Bg Govt, 5–3–1847. Bg Med B to Govt, 20–10–1847.

56 Bg Asy Report, 31–3–1852.

57 J. Macpherson, 'Report on Insanity among Europeans in Bengal, founded on the experience of the Calcutta Lunatic Asylum', review in *Calcutta Review* 26 (1856): 607.

58 Minute by Govr Falkland, Bombay, 7–9–1850.

59 Act XXXVI of 1858, Section 4.

60 Act IV of 1849 was modelled on: 39 & 40 Geo III, c. 94; 1 & 2 Vic, c. 14; 3 & 4 Vic, c. 54. Acts XXXIV, XXXV, XXXVI of 1858 were modelled on: 16 & 17 Vict, c.70,96,97. Act 14 & 15 Vict, c. 81 integrated: 39 & 40 Geo III, c. 94.

61 *A Grenadier's Diary*, 1842–1856 (London: India Office Library and Records, manuscripts).

62 Minute by I. E. Drinkwater Bethune, Leg C of India, 10–6–1848. Minute by Bethune, Leg C of India, 30–6–1848.

63 Minute by I. E. Drinkwater Bethune, Leg C of India, 10–6–1848. Minute by Bethune, Leg C of India, 30–6–1848.

64 Minute by Lord Dalhousie, Leg C of India, 16–6–1848.

65 Minute by I. E. Drinkwater Bethune, Leg C of India, 10–6–1848. Minute by Bethune, Leg C of India, 30–6–1848. Minute by Lord Dalhousie, Leg C of India, 16–6–1848.

66 Minute by Lord Dalhousie, Leg C of India, 16–6–1848.

67 See also W. Ll. Parry-Jones, *The Trade in Lunacy. A study of private madhouses in England* in *the eighteenth and nineteenth centuries* (London: Routledge & Kegan Paul 1972), pp. 64–70.

68 Macpherson, *Report on Insanity*, p. 596.

69 Minute by Govr Falkland, Bombay, 7–9–1850.

70 Table shewing the number of public patients treated in the Lunatic Asylum at Bhowanipore, and the results from 1 January 1824 to 30 December 1850. Bm Asy Report, 31–3–1852.

Chapter 3: The Institutions

1 W. Ernst, *Psychiatry and Colonialism: The Treatment of European Lunatics in British India, 1800–1858* (University of London, School of Oriental and African Studies: unpublished PhD thesis, 1986).

2 *Records of Pembroke House and Ealing Lunatic Asylum, 1818–1892* (London: India Office Library and Records), Medical Certificates, Case Books.

3 W. Ernst, 'The Establishment of "Native Lunatic Asylums" in early nineteenth-century British India', in G. J. Meulenbeld and D. Wujastyk, (eds), *Studies on Indian Medical History* (Groningen: Egbert Forsten 1987), p. 198.

4 J. MacPherson, 'Report on Insanity among Europeans in Bengal, founded on the experience of the Calcutta Lunatic Asylum', review in *Calcutta Review*, 26 (1856): 595f.

5 Minute Govr Falkland, Bombay, 7–9–1850.

6 *Census of the Island of Bombay* (Bombay: Education Society Press, 1864), p. II.

7 *Memorandum on the Census of British India of* 1871–72 (London: Eyre and Spottiswoode 1875), p. 37.

8 Bg Med B to Govt, 27–3–1851.

9 J. MacPherson, *Report on Insanity. Royal Commission on the Sanitary State of the Army* in *India* (London: Eyre & Spottiswoode for HMSO 1863), vol. 1, p. 592. Bg Med B to Govt, 20–10–1847.

10 W. Ernst, 'A Case of Intellectual Insanity', *History of Psychiatry* 1, no. 2 (1990): 207–22.

11 MacPherson, *Report on Insanity*, p. 603.

12 MacPherson, *Report on Insanity*, p. 603, footnote.

13 *Royal Commission*, p. 592 (data apply to Bengal Infantry).

14 Bg Jud D, 25–4–1806.

15 Md Mil L, 18–2–1794.

16 Md Mil B to Govt, 16–7–1844. Md Jud L, 3–1–1845. Md Mil B to G-i-C, 28–8–1846.

17 Bg Med B to Govt, 20–10–1847.

18 Bg Med B to Govt, 10–3–1851.

19 Acc Gen to Bg Govt, 21–3–1850.

20 Bg Accountant Gen to Govt, 21–3–1850.

21 Further Minute Govr Falkland, Bombay, 2–11–1849.

22 E. Eden, *Up the Country* (London and Dublin: Curzon 1978 [1866]), pp. 36, 41, 59, 84.

23 Asy Sup to Bm Govt, 20–2–1850.

24 G. Aberigh-Mackay, *Twenty-one Days in India. Being the Tour of Sir Ali Baba, K.G.B.* (London: Thacker 1902 [1880]), p. 184f.

25 Madras Citizens to Govt, 28–11–1851.

26 Bm Med B to Govt, 3–9–1853.

27 T. H. Thornton and J. L. Kipling, *Lahore* (Lahore: Govt Civil Secretariat Press 1876). H. R. Goulding, *Old Lahore. Reminiscence of a Resident* (Lahore: Universal Books 197– [1924]).

28 MacPherson, *Report on Insanity*, p. 605.

29 H. C. Burdett, *Hospitals and Asylums of the World: Their Origin, History, Construction, Administration, Management, and Legislation*, 3 vols. (London: Churchill 1891–3, 1902), 2: 62.

30 Asy Sup to Bm Med B, 28–2–1850.

31 Bm Asy Report, 31–3–1852.

32 Asy Sup to Bm Med B, 28–2–1850.

33 There prevailed prejudice towards Southern-European people, as indicated by the failure to designate 'Portuguese' as 'European'. The concepts of 'nation-state', 'citizenship' and 'nationality' were also not yet concisely circumscribed. See also V. G. Kiernan, *The Lords of Human Kind. European Attitudes to the Outside World in the Imperial Age* (Harmondsworth: Penguin 1972 [1969]), p. 29.

34 Asy Sup to Bm Med B, 28–2–1850.

35 Suptdg Surgeon Presidency to Md Med B, 23–1–1846.

36 Asy Sup to Suptdg Surg, Md Presidency, 15–7–1846.

37 Md Med B to Govt, 23–7–1846.

38 Md Mil B to C-i-C, 28–8–1846.

39 Md Mil Proc, 29–9–1846.

40 Bg Med B to Govt, 20–10–1847.

41 Bg Med B to Govt, 1–7–1820.

42 Munro to his sister, 1795, quoted in E. Stokes, *The English Utilitarians and India* (Delhi: Oxford University Press 1982 [1959]), p. 25.

43 Elphinstone to Select Committee on Indian Affairs, 1832, cf. Stokes, *English Utilitarians*, p. 25.

44 Bg Asy Report, 14–6–1856.

45 Bg Asy Report, 14–6–1856.

46 Bg Asy Report, 14–6–1856.

47 Bg Med B to Govt, 1856.

48 Bg Asy Report, 14–6–1856.

49 Bg Med B to Govt, 31–5–1836.

50 Bg Asy Report, 14–6–1856.

51 Bg Hosp B to Govt, 26–1–1789.

52 Bm Med B to Govt, 18–3–1801.

53 M. Foucault, quoted in P. Sedgwick, *Psycho Politics* (London: Pluto 1982), p 133.

54 Bg Asy Report, 14–6–1856.

55 Chief Mag and Supt Police to Md Mil B, 21–8–1852.

56 Bm Asy Report, 31–3–1852.

57 The needs presented by people with what has been termed intellectual disability or mental retardation are complex, so that no one single 'label' can adequately describe this group of people. In addition, some classification systems have been dimensional and some categorical, and reliance is no longer placed on IQ levels by themselves. There have been some recent changes in the terminology used by major agencies in this field. So, for example the American Association on Mental Retardation changed its terminology in 2007, replacing mental retardation with the term 'intellectual and developmental disabilities', and the WHO published in 2001 the International Classification of Functioning, Disabilities and Health (ICF), replacing earlier classificatory systems of the WHO. In these circumstances, while the term 'mental retardation' remains in the American DSM-IV classification, the term 'intellectual disability' is more widely used in European English-language professional and academic publications. A. J. Holland 'Classification, diagnosis and needs assessment: in section 10 on intellectual disability (mental retardation)', in M. G. Gelder et al. *New Oxford Textbook of Psychiatry* (Oxford: Oxford university Press 2009), pp. 1819–1824.

58 Asy Supt to Bm Med B, 28–2–1850.

59 Asy Supt to Bm Med B, 28–2–1850.

60 Asy Supt to Bm Med B, 28–2–1850.

61 Asy Supt to Bm Med B, 28–2–1850.

62 Bm Asy Report, 31–3–1852.

63 Bm Asy Report, 31–3–1852.

64 W. Ernst and D. Kantowsky, 'Mad Tales from the Raj. Case Studies from Pembroke House and Ealing Lunatic Asylum, 1818–1892', *Transaction/SOCIETY* 3 (1985): 31–8.

65 Bg Med B to Govt, 20–10–1847.

66 Bg Pub D, 28–6–1820.

67 Bg Med B to Govt, 5–2–1821.

68 Bg Asy Report, 14–6–1856.

69 Bg Asy Report, 14–6–1856.

70 Bg Asy Report, 14–6–1856.

71 Bg Med B to Govt, 31–5–1836.

72 Asy Sup to Bg Med B, 9–4–1856.

73 Bg Med B to Govt, 4–5–1836. Bg Med B to Govt, 7–.5–1836.

74 Bg Asy Report, 14–6–1856.

75 Bg Asy Report, 14–6–1856.

76 Bg Asy Report, 14–6–1856.

77 S. Milligan, cf. C. Allen, *Plain Tales from the Raj. Images of British India in the twentieth century* (London: Macdonald Futura 1981 [1975]), p. 148.

78 See for details on medical treatment Chapter 6.

79 P. Spear, *The Nabobs. A Study of the Social Life of the English in eighteenth-century India* (London and Dublin: Curzon 1980 [1932]), p. 3.

80 W. Ll. Parry-Jones, *The Trade in Lunacy. A Study of Private Madhouses in England in the eighteenth and nineteenth Centuries* (London: Routledge & Kegan Paul 1972), pp. 329, 324, 327.

81 Summary of Correspondence relative to the Calcutta Asylum for Insane Persons, Undersec to Bg Govt, 30–12–1847.
82 Note by Sec to Bg Govt, 9–6–1852.
83 Bg Med B to Govt, 20–10–1847. Note, Accountant's Office, n.d. (1851?).
84 *Summary of Correspondence*, 30–12–1847.
85 Bg Med B to Govt, 27–3–1851.
86 Note by Sec to Bg Govt, 9–6–1852.
87 Parry-Jones, *Trade in Lunacy*, pp. 200f.
88 Note by Sec to Bg Govt, 9–6–1852. Bg Med B to Govt, 10–3–1851.
89 Bg Med B to Govt, 10–3–1851.
90 Parry-Jones, *Trade in Lunacy*, pp. 212ff. Bg Jud D, 4–2–1852.
91 *Summary of Correspondence*, 30–12–1847.
92 Bm Asy Report, 31–3–1852.

Chapter 4: The Medical Profession

1 W. L. Parry-Jones, *The Trade in Lunacy* (London: Routledge & Kegan Paul 1972), p. 84.
2 A. Halliday, *A General View of the Present State of Lunatics, and Lunatic Asylums, in Great Britain and Ireland, and in some other Kingdoms* (London: Underwood 1827), p. 7.
3 J. Conolly, 1830, quoted in Parry-Jones, *Trade in Lunacy*, p. 84.
4 J. M. Granville, 1877, quoted in A. T. Scull, *Museums of Madness* (Harmondsworth: Penguin Books 1982 [1979]), p. 166.
5 W. B. Beatson, 'The Indian Medical Service, Past and Present', review in *British Medical Journal* 2 (1902): 1182.
6 D. MacDonald, *Surgeons Twoe and a Barber. Being some Account of the Life and Work of the Indian Medical Service (1600–1947)* (London: Heinemann 1950), p. 90.
7 MacDonald, *Surgeons Twoe*, p. 11.
8 MacDonald, *Surgeons Twoe*, pp. 86 ff.
9 D. MacDonald, 'The Indian Medical Service. A short account of its achievements. 1600–1947', *Proceedings of the Royal Society Medicine* 49 (1956): 15.
10 MacDonald, *Surgeons Twoe*, p. 86.
11 MacDonald, *Surgeons Twoe*, p. 90.
12 Md Mil D, 20–8–1823.
13 F. Winslow, 1858; quoted in Parry-Jones, *Trade in Lunacy*, p. 88.
14 J. Conolly, 1830; quoted in Parry-Jones, *Trade in Lunacy*, p. 84.
15 Bg Med B to Govt, 31–5–1836.
16 Reference of Ass Surg Adam, 5–3–1821.
17 Quoted in Beardsmore to Bg Govt, 5–5–1836.
18 Bg Med B to Govt, 1–7–1820.
19 J. Sawers to Bg Med, 25–7–1820.
20 MacDonald, *Surgeons Twoe*, p. 109.
21 In 1790 the first Medical Society was founded in Bombay. Not much is known about its members' activities and it can be assumed that its professional leverage was not very great. This slowly changed with the establishment of the Medical and Physical Society of Bombay (1838), which became particularly renowned for its *Transactions*. In 1845 the Grant Medical College was opened. Finally, the Bombay branch of the British Medical Association was established in 1889. See D. G. Crawford, *A History of the Indian Medical Service, 1600–1913* 2 vols. (London: Thacker 1914), 2: 454–5.

22 In 1855 aspirants to the medical service were required to have a command of surgery, of medicine, 'including the diseases of women and children, therapeutics, pharmacy, and hygiene', of anatomy and physiology, and of natural history, including botany and zoology. MacDonald, *Surgeons Twoe*, pp. 109ff.

23 J. M'Cosh, *Medical Advice to the Indian Stranger* (London: W. H. Allen & Co 1841), p. 20.

24 M'Cosh, *Medical Advice*, p. 42.

25 M'Cosh, *Medical Advice*, p. 20.

26 J. C. Bucknill and D. H. Tuke, 1858; J. M. Granville, 1877; cf. Scull, *Museums of Madness*, p. 166.

27 W. F. Bynum, 'Rationales for therapy in British psychiatry, 1780–1835', *Medical History* 18 (1974): 323.

28 G. Higgins, 1816, quoted in Scull, *Museums of Madness*, p. 140.

29 T. Monro, 1815, quoted in Scull, *Museums of Madness*, p. 137.

30 Bynum, *Rationales*, p. 325.

31 W. Battie, 1758, quoted in R. Porter, 'The history of institutional psychiatry in Europe', unpublished typescript.

32 Bg Med B to Govt, 20–10–1847.

33 Bg Med B to Govt, 2–4–1855.

34 M'Cosh, *Medical Advice*, p. 5.

35 M'Cosh, *Medical Advice*, p. 12.

36 M'Cosh, *Medical Advice*, p. 6.

37 M'Cosh, *Medical Advice*, p. 12.

38 Bm Mil D, 1826.

39 L. D. Smith, 'Behind Closed Doors; Lunatic Asylum Keepers, 1800–60', *Social History of Medicine* 1, no. 3 (1988): 309.

40 A. T. Scull, 'Mad-Doctors and Magistrates: English Psychiatry's Struggle for Professional Autonomy in the Nineteenth Century', *European Journal of Sociology* 17 (1976): 279–305.

41 J. Conolly, 1856; quoted in Smith, *Behind Closed Doors*, p. 302.

42 D. Arnold, 'Medical Priorities and Practices in nineteenth-century British India', *South Asia Research*, 5 (1985): 168.

43 M'Cosh, *Medical Advice*, p. 32.

44 M'Cosh, *Medical Advice*, p. 32.

45 Cambridge, Centre of South Asian Studies, Mrs R. Montgomery, Kanpur 7–6–1931.

46 *Royal Commission on the Sanitary State of the Army in India* (London: Eyre and Spottiswoode for HMSO 1863), p. XV.

47 J. R. Martin, 1835, quoted in Arnold, *Medical Priorities*, p. 9.

48 *Royal Commission*, p. XV.

49 D. Arnold, 'Cholera and Colonialism in British India', *Past and Present* 113 (1986): 127.

50 *Royal Commission*, p. XVII.

51 *Royal Commission*, p. XXX.

Chapter 5: The Patients

1 *Records of Pembroke House and Ealing Lunatic Asylum*, Medical Certificates, 1845. Medical history of E. C. Z., 13–12–1844.

2 *Pembroke House*, Med Cert, 1845; Medical history of E.C. Z. by Ass Surg J.F. Morier, 9–12–1844.

3 *Pembroke House*, Med Cert, 1843; case of Private T. C.

4 *Pembroke House*, Med Cert, 1843; case of Gunner P. L.

5 *Pembroke House*, Med Cert, 1843; case of Private J. B.

6 *Pembroke House*, Med Cert, 1843; case of Gunner T. H.

7 Charge of E. C. Z. by Sup Indian Navy, Bombay, 9–11–1839.

8 Records of Service for Indian Navy Officers, 1838–48; E. C. Z.

9 Sec to Govt, Bombay, 1–1–1840.

10 *Pembroke House*, Med Cert, 1846; case of Gunner D. B.

11 *Pembroke House*, Med Cert, 1843; case of Private W. W.

12 *Pembroke House*, Med Cert, 1843; case of Lieutenant J. H. H.

13 Whitehall to India Board, 22–11–1856.

14 Certificate of Dr French, Haileybury, 16–6–1855.

15 Court of Directors to Board of Control, 7–8–1856.

16 J. W. J. O. to India House, 31–8–1855.

17 Certificate of Sir R. Martin, 21–6–1855.

18 Whitehall to India Board, 22–11–1856.

19 India House to O., 7–5–1857.

20 Address by E. C. Z. to Court, Bombay, 1839.

21 Bm Asy Report, 31–3–1852, Appendix.

22 Md Asy Report, 14–3–1808.

23 Bg Med B to Govt, 20–10–1847.

24 *Royal Commission on the Sanitary State of the Army in India* (London: Eyre and Spottiswoode for HMSO 1863), 1: XXIV.

25 Beardsmore to Bg Govt, 23–8–1820.

26 Md Med B to Govt, 15–2–1808.

27 *Pembroke House*, Med Cert, 1843; case of J. K.

28 E. J. Hobsbawm, *Industry and Empire* (Harmondsworth: Penguin Books 1981 [1968]), p. 94. *Pembroke House*, Med Cert, 1843; case of J. K.

29 *The East India Register and Army List* (London: Allen), February 1819.

30 Bg Med B to Govt, 10–3–1851.

31 Bg Asy Report, 14–6–1856; Summary of correspondence relative to the Calcutta Asylum for Insane Persons, Undersec to Bg Govt, 30–12–1847; Annual Return of Patients treated in the Asylum for European Insanes at Bhowanipore during the year 1859, 1–1–1860.

32 *Pembroke House*, Med Cert, 1853; case of F. H.

33 *Pembroke House*, Med Cert, 1845; case of F. P. T.

34 *Pembroke House*, Med Cert, 1845; case of E. C. Z.

35 *Pembroke House*, Med Cert, 1843; case of J. T.

36 *Royal Commission*, p. 755.

37 *Royal Commission*, p. 592.

38 Bm Asy Report, 31–3–1852.

Chapter 6: Medical Theories and Practices

1 W. F. Bynum, 'Psychiatry in its historical context', in M. Shepherd and O. L. Zangwill, *Handbook of Psychiatry* (Cambridge: Cambridge University Press 1982), 1: 24.

2 R. Porter, 'Was there a moral therapy in eighteenth century psychiatry?', *Lynchnos* nn (1981–2): 12–26. R. Porter, 'In the eighteenth century were lunatic asylums total institutions?', *Ego: Bulletin of the Department of Psychiatry, Guy's Hospital* 4 (1983): 12–34.

3 J. Locke, 'An essay concerning humane understanding' (1690), in R. Hunter and I. Macalpine, *Three Hundred Years of Psychiatry, 1535–1850: A History presented in selected English Texts* (London: Oxford University Press 1963), p. 237.

4 R. Porter, 'Being Mad in Georgian England', *History Today* 31 (1981): 42–48.

5 Bg Med B to Govt, 30–11–1818.

6 Bm Med B to Govt, 24–5–1853.

7 Bynum, *Psychiatry in its historical context*, p. 26.

8 *Records of Pembroke House and Ealing Lunatic Asylums*, Medical Certificates, 1854; case of Private G. T.

9 Asy Sup to Bm Med B, 28–2–1851.

10 *Memorandum on the Census of British India of* 1871–72 (London: Eyre and Spottiswoode 1875), p. 37.

11 Asy Sup to Bg Govt, 14–6–1856.

12 J. MacPherson, 'Report on Insanity among Europeans in Bengal, founded on the experience of the Calcutta Lunatic Asylum', review in *Calcutta Review* 26 (1856): 593.

13 Bg Med B to Govt, 30–11–1818.

14 D. MacPherson, quoting R. Martin, in *Royal Commission on the Sanitary State of the Army in India* (London: Eyre and Spottiswoode for HMSO 1863), vol. 2, Appendix, p. 640. R. Martin, in *Royal Commission*, vol. 1, p. 10 (PS).

15 R. Martin, in *Royal Commission*, vol. 1, p. 10 (PS).

16 Bg Med B to Govt, 20–10–1847.

17 W. A. Green, 'Contributions towards the pathology of Insanity in India', *The Indian Annals of Medical Science or half-yearly journal on practical medicine and surgery* 4 (1857): 374–435.

18 Green, *Contributions*, p. 376.

19 Sup Bhowanipur and Dhalanda Lun Asy to Med Dep, Bengal, 8–5–1858.

20 Green, *Contributions*, p. 375.

21 Sup Bhowanipur and Dhalanda Lun Asy to Med Dep, Bengal, 8–5–1858.

22 L. J. Ray, 'Models of Madness in Victorian Asylum Practice', *European Journal of Sociology* 22 (1981): 229–63.

23 Maudsley quoting Bucknill, in V. Skultans, *Madness and Morals* (London: Routledge and Kegan Paul 1975), p. 6.

24 K. Ballhatchet, *Race, Sex and Class under the Raj. Imperial Attitudes and Policies and their Critics, 1793–1905* (London: Weidenfeld and Nicolson 1980), p. 7.

25 Ray, *Models of Madness*.

26 Sup Bhowanipur and Dhalanda Lunatic Asy to Med Dep, Bengal, 8–5–1858.

27 Asy Sup to Bm Govt, 31–3–1852.

28 Asy Sup to Bm Govt, 31–3–1849.

29 *Pembroke House*, Med Cert, 1818–1892.

30 Editorial preface to *Transactions of the Medical and Physical Society Bombay*, 1 (1838): IX-X.

31 *Pembroke House*, Med Cert, 1860; case of able seaman Charles C.

32 Md Med B to Govt, 8–1–1820. Md Med B to Govt, 29–3–1802.

33 Md Med B to Govt, 8–1–1820.

34 Md Med B to Govt, 8–1–1820.

35 *Pembroke House*, Med Cert, 1860; case of able seaman Charles C., case report, surgeon general hospital, Calcutta, no date.

36 *Pembroke House*, Med Cert, Charles C.

37 *Pembroke House*, Med Cert, Charles C.

38 *Pembroke House*, Med Cert, Charles C.; Continuation of case report, Sup of Bhowanipur Asy, 15–2–1860.

39 *Pembroke House*, Med Cert, Charles C.; Continuation of case report.

40 *Pembroke House*, Med Cert, Charles C.; Continuation of case report.

41 See the title of G. Hill's 'Lecture': R. G. Hill, 'Total abolition of personal restraint in the treatment of the insane. A lecture on the management of lunatic asylums, and the treatment of the insane; delivered at the Mechanics' Institution, Lincoln, on the 21st of June, 1838, etc', in Hunter and Macalpine, *Three Hundred Years*, p. 886.

42 Hill, *Total abolition*, p. 892.

43 Asy Sup to Dir Gen Med Dep, Bengal, 8–5–1858.

44 Asy Sup to Dir Gen Med Dep, Bengal, 8–5–1858.

45 Asy Sup to Dir Gen Med Dep, Bengal, 8–5–1858.

46 Asy Sup to Dir Gen Med Dep, Bengal, 8–5–1858.

47 Asy Sup to Dir Gen Med Dep, Bengal, 8–5–1858.

48 Asy Sup to Dir Gen Med Dep, Bengal, 8–5–1858.

49 Asy Sup to Dir Gen Med Dep, Bengal, 8–5–1858.

50 Asy Sup to Dir Gen Med Dep, Bengal, 8–5–1858.

51 Minute by Second Member of Med B, Madras, 4–3–1808.

52 J Reid, 1808, quoted in R. Porter, 'The History of Institutional Psychiatry in Europe', unpublished typescript.

53 Bentinck to Metcalfe, 16–9–1829, and to Mancy, 1–6–1834; quoted in P. Spear, *The Oxford History of Modern India, 1740–1975* (Delhi: Oxford University Press 1984 [1965]), p. 145.

54 Green, *Contributions*, pp. 374–5.

55 Green, *Contributions*, pp. 375–6.

56 J. R. Miller, M.D., Surgeon, 'Annual Report of the 23rd Regt Native Light Infantry', *Transactions of the Medical and Physical Society, Bombay* 4 (1857–8): 274.

57 Macpherson, *Report on Insanity*, p. 598.

58 F. S. Arnott, M. D., Surgeon 'Report on the Health of the 1st Bombay European Regiment', *Transactions of the Medical and Physical Society of Bombay* 2 (1855): 157.

59 A. S. Thomson, M. D., 'Could the Natives of a temperate climate colonize and increase in a tropical country and vice versa?', *Transactions of the Medical and Physical Society of Bombay* 6 (1843): 112–37.

60 Thomson, *Natives of a temperate climate*, pp. 112–37. See also D. Arnold, 'White Colonization and Labour in nineteenth-century India', *Journal of Imperial and Commonwealth History* 2 (1983): 133–58.

61 Thomson, *Natives of a temperate climate*, p. 113.

62 Thomson, *Natives of a temperate climate*, p. 114–15.

63 Thomson, *Natives of a temperate climate*, p. 116.

64 *Pembroke House*, Med Cert, 1852; case of H. S.

Chapter 7: Conclusion: 'Mad Dogs and Englishmen...'

1 M. Foucault, *Folie et Déraison. Histoire de la folie à l'âge classique* (Paris: Librairie Plon 1961), p. VII. 'Faire l'histoire de la folie, voudra...dire: faire une étude structurale de l'ensemble historique – notions institutions, mesures juridiques et policières, concepts scientifiques – qui tient captive une folie dont l'état sauvage ne peut jamais être restitue en lui-même.' Foucault then goes on to claim: 'a défaut de cette inaccessible pureté primitive, l'étude

structurale doit remonter vers la décision qui lie et sépare à la fois raison et folie; elle doit tendre à découvrir l'échange perpétuel, l'obscure racine commune, l'affrontement originaire qui donne sens a l'unité aussi bien qu'a l'opposition du sens et de l'insensé'.

2 Report Bm Lun Asy, 31–3–1852.

3 K Ballhatchet, *Race, Sex and Class under the Raj. Imperial Attitudes and Policies and their Critics, 1793–1905* (London: Weidenfeld and Nicolson 1980), p. 3.

4 G. Balandier, 1951, quoted in D. Frigessi Castelnuovo and M. Risso, *Emigration und Nostalgie. Sozialgeschichte, Theorie und Mythos psychischer Krankheit von Auswanderern* (Frankfurt am Main: Cooperative-Verlag 1986), p. 145. (orig. edn: *A mezza parete. Emigrazione, nostalgia, malattia mentale* (Torino: Giulio Einaudi editore 1982).

INDEX

Lightning Source UK Ltd.
Milton Keynes UK
16 March 2010

151490UK00002B/15/P